*Hans-Jürgen Martin*

# Zebra Finches

Everything about Housing, Care, Nutrition, Breeding, and Disease

Special Chapter: Understanding Zebra Finches

*Edited by* Dr. Matthew M. Vriends

With Color Photographs by Outstanding
Animal Photographers
and Drawings by Gertrud Thomas

Barron's

First English language edition published in 1985 by
Barron's Educational Series, Inc.
© 1984 by Grafe and Unzer GmbH, Munich, West
Germany.

The title of the German edition is *Zebrafinken*.

Translated by Rita and Robert Kimber

*All inquiries should be addressed to:*
Barron's Educational Series, Inc.
250 Wireless Boulevard
Hauppauge, New York 11788

*Library of Congress Catalog Card No. 85-1336*

International Standard Book No. 0-8120-3497-X

Library of Congress Cataloging in Publication Data

Martin, Hans-Jürgen.
  Zebra finches.

  Translation of: Zebrafinken.
  Includes index.
  1. Zebra finch.  I. Title.
SF473.Z42M3713  1985    636.6'862    85-1336
ISBN 0-8120-3497-X

Printed in Hong Kong
456    490    17 16 15 14

Front cover: A pair of Gray Zebra Finches; female
(left), male (right).
Inside front cover: Young Zebra Finch hen perching
on a rack filled with nesting material.
Inside back cover: Young Zebra Finches whose bills
are still black.
Back cover: Zebra Finches in their native habitat in
Australia.

*Photographs*
Angermayer: front cover
Bielfeld: page 28 (lower left and right)
Martin: inside front cover; pages 17, 18, 46; inside
back cover
Oppenborn: pages 28 (upper left and right, middle
right), 27
Reinhard: page 45
Schrempp: page 28 (middle left)
Schweiger: pages 63, 64; back cover.

*Important Notes*
The subject of this book is how to take care of Zebra
Finches in captivity. In dealing with these birds, always
remember that newly purchased birds — even when they
appear perfectly healthy — may well be carriers of sal-
monellae. This is why it is highly advisable to have
sample droppings analyzed and to observe strict hygienic
rules. Other infectious diseases that can endanger humans, are rare in Zebra Finches. Still, if you see a doctor
because you or a member of your household has symptoms of a cold or the flu, mention that you keep birds. No
one who is allergic to feathers or feather dust should keep
birds. If you have any doubts, consult your physician
before you buy a bird.

# Contents

# *Preface*

Exotic finches populate the cages and aviaries of a great many bird lovers because hardly anyone is immune to the charm of these colorful birds. And if a popularity contest were held for cage birds, the Zebra Finch would surely be among the top winners. This Australian grass finch is so popular not only because it looks pretty but also because even in captivity it follows its natural reproductive behavior, starting with the courtship displays of mating and progressing to the busy activity of raising young.

Zebra Finches are extremely social birds that must have another member of their species for a partner, and they therefore have to be kept in pairs. In their native Australia they gather in large flocks that stay together to search for food, and they breed in semi-arid regions as well as in all kinds of cultivated land, including gardens. The natural behavior patterns of these birds—that is, the close bonding between mates and a strong nesting instinct—largely account for the fact that aviculturists have been able to breed these birds without problem for over a hundred years. All the Zebra Finches for sale at pet stores have been bred in captivity, so that a pet owner does not have to worry about acclimating difficulties—difficulties that are often encountered with birds born in the wild.

In this little book, the author, Hans-Jürgen Martin, has gathered everything Zebra Finch owners need to know to keep and care for their pets properly, and in the extensive chapter on reproduction and breeding of Zebra Finches even an experienced aviculturist will find much new infor-

mation. The author has been raising Zebra Finches for many years with great success, and he has studied in depth all the questions connected with the proper care of these birds. He presents advice based on practical experience in a clear and informative manner and discusses all important topics, such as purchase, appropriate housing, diet, and breeding.

In the special chapter "Understanding Zebra Finches," the author describes the way of life and the behavior of Zebra Finches living in the wild in their native Australia. This chapter is based primarily on the publications of Dr. Klaus Immelmann, Professor of Biology at the University of Bielefeld (Germany) and Director of the Institute for Ethology. We are also indebted to Dr. Immelmann for reading the manuscript of this pet owner's guide and offering valuable criticisms and suggestions. Dr. Immelmann, who is considered the foremost expert in the German-speaking world on Zebra Finches, has traveled a number of times to Australia, where he has devoted considerable study to the behavior of Zebra Finches.

The drawings by Gertrud Thomas, who has Zebra Finches herself, and the color photos—especially those of Zebra Finches in their natural habitat taken by the two well-known animal photographers Arendt and Schweiger and published here for the first time—enhance the informational value of the book. The author, too, has contributed some exceptional color photos, such as the series of pictures illustrating behavior and the shots of nestling during their first days of life.

# Considerations Before You Buy

## Zebra Finches as Pets

Zebra Finches have long been among the most popular cage birds, because they, along with Java Sparrows and Society Finches, are the easiest of all the exotic finches to keep and breed.

But before you let yourself be tempted to buy a pair of these pretty and lively Australian birds, you should take into account that even though they have been bred in aviaries and kept in people's homes for over one hundred years, Zebra Finches have to a large extent retained the behavior of wild birds. Thus a Zebra Finch does not have the calm manner of a canary or a budgerigar but, like Waxbills, Mannikins, Munias, and allied species (*Estrildidae*), has a noticeably greater need for movement and keeps a greater distance from humans, whom it will not and cannot accept as substitute partners in the absence of other members of its species. In other words, Zebra Finches are not as friendly and capable of learning as canaries, budgies, or parrots. And anyone who wants a pet for touching and stroking should choose a mammal (cat, dog, etc.) rather than a bird.

Another factor to consider is that Zebra Finches naturally live in flocks. On their home continent of Australia they live and breed year round in large flocks that form as the birds search for food and water. Zebra Finches are social animals that need the presence of others of their kind at all times (p. 69). It is advisable to keep more than just one pair if you have a large enough aviary. The marked social behavior of these exotic finches is displayed fully only if they are in a group; a miniflock of three or four pairs is therefore a good compromise. In such a situation there will never be a dull moment; there will always be a neighbor to visit, a nesting site to defend, or a small concert to be given.

But as an interested bird-watcher you will derive a lot of pleasure even from one pair, provided you restrict yourself to watching and do not expect too much of your charges. Never hope for special appreciation for the chores you perform for your birds. Indeed, they would be delighted if you could do the cleaning and feeding without getting too close to them.

Zebra Finches are ideal subjects for the hobbyist who wants to study animal behavior, especially if you work outside the home. The birds will not miss you while you are away at work, and when you come home you can slowly become familiar with all their natural behavior patterns and especially with their way of reproducing and raising their young. Because they are domesticated, Zebra Finches are better suited for observation than are any other exotic finches, some of which are extremely shy.

In Zebra Finches it is easy to tell the male (left) from the female (right). The male has orange cheeks and spots on the sides of the body.

5

# Considerations Before You Buy

## Are You Sure Zebra Finches Are for You?

As a friend of animals, you will no doubt want to keep your birds in a manner that suits their nature. But do you know exactly what the needs of Zebra Finches are? You should select these birds only if you can answer all the following questions with an unqualified yes.

• Do you know that Zebra Finches—unlike budgerigars and canaries—always stay relatively wild and shy? They can therefore never be hand tamed.

• Are you aware that Zebra Finches (like all *Estrildidae* species) cannot be kept singly? Since these birds cannot become attached to humans, a Zebra Finch that is kept by itself misses very acutely the company of others of its kind and suffers from loneliness even more than many other (larger) cage birds. The results are disturbed behavior, susceptibility to illness, and, all too frequently, death.

• Are you able to house two or more Zebra Finches properly? In spite of their small size, these lively creatures always need plenty of room to fly, requiring a large flight cage at the least, which will not be inexpensive (p. 9).

• Are you able to house your birds in a room where they will not be bothered by loud music or by television, and especially where they will not be exposed to cigarette smoke?

• Will the birds be well taken care of if you go away on a trip or have to go to the hospital?

• Do you have at least half an hour a day that you can devote to your birds (p. 32)?

• Are you willing to put up with the dirt your birds will generate every day? Zebra Finches are tiny creatures, but they still lose feathers and feather dust and scatter empty seed husks and sand all about. Even the most generous accommodations will not prevent this. And you cannot train the birds to change their ways.

• Are you sure that you—and the other members of your family—are not allergic to feathers or bird droppings? If there is any question about this in your mind, check with your doctor.

• Do all the other members of your household approve of your plans? Many people react negatively to the constant fluttering or the singing of birds.

• Have you given some thought to the problem of baby birds? A compatible pair of Zebra Finches is practically impossible to keep from producing offspring. The fledglings, of course, demand some special attention as well as additional space, and you will finally have to find homes for them (p. 39).

## Where You Can Purchase Zebra Finches

If you want to buy Zebra Finches, you have two alternatives:

• You can buy your birds at a pet shop or the pet section of a department store. There you will often have a chance to choose from among a larger number of birds. But you can never be entirely certain that a given pair is not related, and the mating of siblings, especially, should be avoided if at all possible.

Zebra Finches offered for sale by pet dealers are generally under one year old. (Under proper care, Zebra Finches can live to about 12 years.)

• You can buy Zebra Finches from an amateur breeder. This makes sense if you are interested in a particular color strain or if you are contemplating breeding birds for show. In this case you should look around at bird shows and get the addresses of successful exhibitors.

I would urge you most strongly not to purchase birds through the mail. You have no say in what birds are actually mailed to you, and there is no telling what state they will be in when they arrive. A sick bird would have to be sent back immediately, a second trip that would mean certain death.

## What to Watch Out for When You Buy

Before choosing your Zebra Finches, you should first look around carefully to see how the birds are housed. A well-run pet shop keeps cage birds in sufficiently large box cages or in aviaries that are always clean and have fresh sand on the bottom. The birds have sufficient light and air as well as fresh, clean food and water.

Unfortunately, there are pet dealers who do not live up to these standards and who keep birds under rather miserable conditions. Be sure, therefore, to buy only strong, healthy birds that are well cared for (p. 8). Do not be deterred by having to spend a few extra dollars. The health of your birds is crucial,

Zebra Finches need a lot of room for flying and are therefore best housed in an aviary.

and a reputable pet shop is most likely to provide you with healthy birds.

The more you yourself know about birds, the better you will be able to tell whether a salesperson knows his or her business and will be able to give you good advice. Of course, an experienced aviculturist could also be of assistance in purchasing birds.

When you observe Zebra Finches, you may spot an adult pair, the two partners sitting next to each other, grooming each other's feathers, and sharing other activities. In such a case, respect the bonding that has already taken place and buy both birds. You will be doing the two a favor, and you can be sure you have a pair that gets along well.

It is quite easy, by the way, to tell males from females by the more colorful plumage the male wears year round. The only similarities in the sexes' gray plumage are a tear line running down from the eye and the black and white bands on the tail (photo on front cover). In the case of White Zebra Finches, however, you have to look at the bill for clues: In males it is usually considerably darker red than in females.

# Considerations Before You Buy

## How to Recognize Healthy Zebra Finches

Even if you are no expert on birds you can tell, by observing certain signs, whether a Zebra Finch is healthy and likely to make good breeding stock.

• **Behavior:** Does the bird that appeals to you seem lively? Does it eat and drink, groom its feathers, and take part in the activities of the other birds? A sick bird usually sits on a perch or on the bottom of the cage with its feathers fluffed up and eyes squeezed shut.

• **Plumage:** The plumage should form a smooth coat and not show any major bare patches. Feathers that are stuck together near the vent indicate some intestinal disorder that is usually caused by improper care or dirty food and water.
If a bird has just taken a bath, its feathers will obviously look a little disheveled. In case of doubt, ask the salesperson to catch the bird and blow against the anal feathers so that you can have a look at the vent.

• **Legs:** Are they straight, smooth, and clean? An abnormal stance indicates a fracture. The horny scales should not stick out, and the full number of toes and toenails have to be present.

• **Body build or "type":** The body should be stocky and teardrop-shaped—broad at the shoulders and wide at the breast—and have a straight back. A clearly bent or forked tail, drooping wings, a concave or convex back, or a prominent breastbone are all defects in type that tend to be passed on hereditarily. If you would like to breed Zebra Finches, you should pay attention to the body build of the birds you choose (p. 50).

## Who Will Look after the Zebra Finches When You Go on Vacation?

Like any other prospective pet owner, you will have to think about who will take care of your Zebra Finches when you are unable to do so yourself. This will be the case primarily when you go on trips, either on vacations or for business. The simplest solution probably is to ask friends, acquaintances, or neighbors to look after the birds while you are gone. Before leaving on a trip, have available a supply of all the different foods the birds eat, and leave the cage or aviary in a meticulous state. Provide the substitute caretaker with detailed instructions (not just oral, but also written) about all the necessary chores and about any problems that might arise. If there is a fancier of exotic finches among your acquaintances, this would obviously be the best person for the job.

Another possibility is to entrust your birds to a pet shop or local animal hospital for a fee while you are gone. Be sure to make inquiries ahead of time. But this solution is far from ideal for your charges. They will be thrust into an entirely new environment and, if used to a large aviary at home, they will have to adjust to a small cage. If the pet shop or your veterinarian is not really close by, you should carry your birds in a small shipping box made of wood or in a cardboard box similar to the one used when you bought the birds.

# Housing and Equipment

## Proper Accommodations for Birds

The most important thing to do before bringing home a pair of birds is to set up accommodations that suit their way of life. If you look around in a pet shop you will find there are all kinds of useful gadgets, but not all of the cages on display will be suitable for Zebra Finches.

Zebra Finches are extremely active, and even though diminutive in size they require plenty of space for flying at all times. Unfortunately, some bird owners still take as their guideline the small cages meant for tame cage birds (canaries and budgerigars, for example) that can spend several hours a day flying free. For pet suppliers, displaying indoor aviaries presents a space problem. In order for a Zebra Finch to be able to fly even a little and not to have to merely hop from perch to perch, a flying distance of at least 20 inches (½ meter) is required. If you take into account how much the perches stick out from the sides of the cage, you have to figure on an overall length of 28 to 32 inches (70 to 80 centimeters). A cage should never be smaller than this and, if at all possible, should be larger. When your birds produce offspring, you will need a bigger cage or will have to have a second cage in reserve (p. 39). Please do not let anyone convince you that Zebra Finches can be kept in a small cage.

The cage should be rectangular in shape, never round. Slanted or round sides are not suitable, nor are peaked or pagoda-like roofs, little alcoves, or unnecessary ornaments typical of the so-called luxury models. For the bird keeper these fancy extras only cost more money and require more time to clean, and for the lively birds the superfluous nooks and angles can easily become the source of serious injuries (see "List of Dangers," p. 34).

When buying a cage or an aviary for Zebra Finches, you always have to make sure that the bars are no more than ½ inch (12 millimeters) apart. Whether the bars run horizontally or vertically does not matter. No part of the cage (grating, bottom pan, food dishes, or other accessories) should be made of brass, because brass forms poisonous verdigris if it comes in contact with moisture (bath water or droppings).

Cages with a removable clean-out drawer at the bottom are very practical. Without such a drawer you have to lift the cage off the bottom tray each time you clean it, not only upsetting your feathered friends in the process but also providing a chance for escape. To preclude the danger of escape, drawers deeper than 1 inch (2.5 centimeters) should be equipped with a flap to cover the opening.

Another useful feature is a partition that can be set up in the cage to discourage animosities between birds.

## Cages and Small Aviaries

Take plenty of time to select a cage or aviary, and do not hesitate to look around in several stores. Larger flight cages that the dealer does not carry in the store can be ordered from catalogs. The market offers a wide range of cages and aviaries, and you will surely be able to find a suitable home for your birds.

# Housing and Equipment

## Metal Cages

Pet stores carry all-metal cages in many sizes and shapes. To prevent rusting, the metal is lacquered, galvanized, or chromed. Only the largest of these cages have even the minimum dimensions of 28 inches (70 centimeters) long and 20 inches (50 centimeters) high required for Zebra Finches. These cages also have the disadvantage of not having solid back walls. A back wall made of grating not only leads to extra dirt to be cleaned up but also deprives the Zebra Finches of a needed feeling of safety. The great argument in favor of these cages is their reasonable price.

## Wooden Cages

Wooden bird cages have a long tradition. They are made of square bars of beech wood, about ⅜ inch (1 centimeter) in diameter, that run between vertical wire bars. Their price is comparable to that of metal cages. The wood is their weak point, because it discolors and will rot if not treated with an appropriate sealer (see "Do-It-Yourself Bird Homes," p. 14).

Usually the floor underneath the drawer consists of a board of pressed wood fiber, which will probably have to be replaced after a while with treated plywood or with plastic or metal.

The great advantage of these wooden cages is that they come with solid back walls and in larger sizes, such as 40 × 16 × 20 inches (100 × 40 × 50 centimeters), which is a convenient size for *one* pair of Zebra Finches that has babies now and then. Zebra Finches living in a cage of these dimensions will not become lethargic or fat, and their young will develop into good fliers.

## Box Cages

Large box-type cages have proved very practical. Since only the front and the top have a grating and the other walls as well as the floor consist of easy-to-clean chipboard covered with a protective layer, the daily droppings and other dirt are largely confined to the cage. In addition, the birds feel very safe inside such a cage. Two perching trees and a clean-out drawer are needed for equipment.

Another type of box cage is the flying and brooding box that is made of synthetic ma-

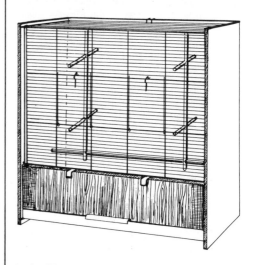

A pair of Zebra Finches would feel comfortable in a box-type cage like this, measuring at least 29 × 18½ × 29½ inches (74 × 46 × 75 cm.).

# Housing and Equipment

terials and has a solid top for the sake of stability. These boxes get no light from the top (p. 15), but they can be stacked, are very easy to keep clean, and come in many sizes and variations.

**Prefabricated Mini-Aviaries**

Small aviaries made of prefabricated units that can be disassembled are highly recommended. They are ideal not only because they can be reduced to relatively small size for transport but also because you can build onto them as need arises with additional parts that come in standard measurements. With a minimum of work you can assemble sides, roof, and floor into a new unit that can be added onto the original aviary. The long flying area created in this way can then, of course, be subdivided by walls of grating.

If you have such a setup, you can make extra room for a new pair of Zebra Finches or for offspring from your birds, and you can provide protection from persecution for young birds that have become independent or for new arrivals.

Pet stores also offer more or less elaborate do-it-yourself kits. How successfully you put them together depends on your manual skills (see "Do-It-Yourself Bird Homes," p. 14).

Many bird fanciers like to have their pets in their living area and therefore want an aviary that looks attractive and fits in with the decor. They can choose from a remarkably varied assortment of spacious and handsome mini-aviaries that are well designed and come in almost every conceivable style. If your birds have a home of generous proportions, they will demonstrate all their natural patterns of behavior and provide you with a fascinating "Zebra Finch program."

Aviaries made entirely of wood or with wooden decorations and built to resemble furniture probably look best in a living room. Depending on the interior decor of your home, you can choose, for instance, between pine and oak finish or opt for heavy trim in mahogany or other fancy wood. Other models are made of anodized aluminum, but these are somewhat more expensive. Many of these aviaries come with stands (some on wheels) made of the same material. Shelves with doors are often built into the stand, giving the whole thing the appearance of a small cupboard and at the same time offering space for accessories.

You can also place a small aviary on a piece of furniture or on a shelf. Models as tall and as long as 5 feet (1.5 meters) and as deep as about 1½ feet (50 centimeters) can still be moved quite easily for spring cleaning or for permanent relocation.

## Indoor Aviaries

By indoor aviaries I mean homes for birds that exceed 40 cubic feet (1½ cubic meters). Such a definition is of course arbitrary, but aviaries of this size approach the size of built-in aviaries or glass cases and can be moved only on wheels, if at all. Usually they are mounted directly on the floor or on a special foundation. This

# Housing and Equipment

means that there are no drawers at the bottom; access for cleaning is through a low door.

Models made of aluminium or galvanized steel can be used outdoors and are available in units of standard measurements. They can therefore be assembled into the size desired and can be expanded.

Consider carefully what the quietest location for your aviary would be and where it would at the same time be displayed to best advantage. The question of place is of course most important for a built-in aviary that cannot later be moved without considerable trouble. An indoor aviary can be custom built for any apartment either by a manufacturer or by an owner handy with tools. A corner aviary consists simply of two large sections of grating and is

therefore quite inexpensive. Make sure there is no wallpaper on the walls that could serve as a haven to pests. A tiled wall can look very attractive and is practical. Cover the floor of the aviary with sand and forest soil (separating the two areas, perhaps, by bricks or stones). You can even set up a shallow "water hole" for the ever-thirsty Zebra Finches. Tree limbs and branches should not intrude into the birds' flying space, and, to prevent contamination by droppings, the branches should not be mounted over food and water dishes. Many

Someone handy with tools could easily build a corner aviary like this, in which several pairs of Zebra Finches could build nests and raise young at the same time. The nesting boxes should be hung as described on page 41.

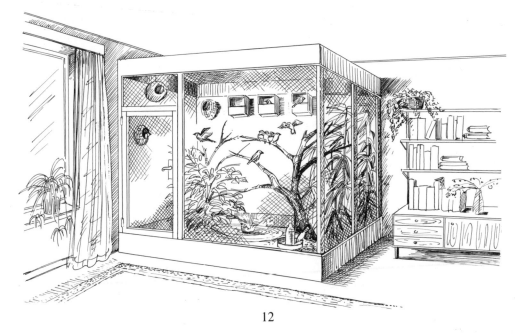

bird keepers like to decorate their aviaries with artificial plants. This is not necessary, but it does the Zebra Finches no harm. Large, thick, smooth leaves can be washed off easily, so that fake ivy or philodendron is preferable to artificial evergreens or ferns.

You can get good ideas on how to set up your aviary from visiting the bird sections of zoos or bird preserves. There is also an entire literature devoted exclusively to questions of planning and building aviaries.

Persons living in a home of their own or in a large condominium also have the option of setting up an entire room for their birds. This way the problem of dirt in the living area is eliminated, but the possibilities for watching the birds are seriously curtailed unless a small observation area is set off or a large glass door is installed between living room and bird room. However, glass represents a hazard for all birds, the reason that all windows and glass doors should be protected with mesh. A window with mesh, when opened, can also serve as a passageway to an outside area (a kind of bay window made of wire mesh or grating) that your Zebra Finches will much enjoy in the summertime.

## A Bird Building or Outdoor Aviary

For an aviculturist who wants to breed birds, a separate, solid birdhouse is ideal because it offers accommodations for many Zebra Finch pairs in separate compartments. Usually a building permit is required for such a structure. In order to provide all the inside compartments with adequate daylight, the wall with the windows, forming one of the long sides of a rectangular bird building, should face south, and some of the roof should be transparent. But even if you use a generous amount of glass and insulation, you will still need artificial light and heat. Square compartments are better than long, narrow ones, which allow the birds to fly only from one end to the other. The compartments should be accessible from a hallway through very low doors, so that the Zebra Finches are less likely to escape. The door leading to the outside should have an air lock on the inside for extra safety.

For drawing up a floor plan as well as for details of actual execution, you should consult literature on the subject and study aviaries in animal parks as models. These bird buildings will often lack windows or glass brick, but they will have planted open-air aviaries on the south side that the birds have access to through little doors. Such an outside area provides not only a welcome change of scenery, with its varied growth of bushes, reeds, and grass, but also fresh air and sunlight.

The soil of an outdoor aviary has to be dug up and replaced periodically, because the accumulated droppings can harbor parasites and disease carriers whose eggs survive even the coldest winters. The foundation for the frames of the wire mesh has to be at least 3 feet (1 meter) deep so that mice and rats cannot dig under it to get into the aviary.

These rules also apply to an open-air aviary with a small attached shelter, a setup that may look appealing to many a Zebra Finch fancier. But I have serious reservations about this type of housing. Zebra Finches are used to a warm, dry climate, and they cannot be acclimated to our cooler latitudes. In some states they can be kept outdoors without risk only for about five months during late spring and summer. It makes little sense to build a spacious outdoor aviary to be used so little and then have to move the birds to a small (heated) indoor aviary for the rest of the year. The reverse is better, namely a sizable building with a smaller outside area.

## Do-It-Yourself Bird Homes

If you have some experience in working with tools, you will have no difficulties in constructing a home for your Zebra Finches. The following tips may help you in building a small aviary.

For the amateur builder, a box-type aviary (p. 10) is clearly the best kind of bird home to construct. A back wall, a floor board, two side walls, and a lower front panel with a flap are screwed together. Clean-out drawers are fitted in—ready-made panels of mesh bought and either attached with hooks or slid into grooves you have previously sawed or rabbeted along the edge of the side walls. Then all that is left to do so is to mount small mop boards of wood or aluminium (molding to prevent food and droppings from falling between the walls and clean-out drawers) and, of course, to plan the interior. Remember in your planning that the wire mesh panels and the baths you buy are standard in size and that you have to build to their exact measurements.

The floor and the back and side walls can be cut to order. Chipboard with protective plastic coatings comes in white or various wood finishes; it is easy to keep clean but fairly heavy. Thick pine boards are lighter, as is plywood. A light veneer sets off the Zebra Finches to best advantage. If you want to be able to take your aviary apart, use insert nuts and screws.

Plain wood has to be sealed against mites, dirt, and rotting. The same is true for commercially made wooden cages (p. 10). Light sealers, particularly with an acrylic base, are suitable for the inside of the cage. You can also use sealers containing solvents if you let the cage air after the final coat for at least three weeks. All the parts that are exposed to a lot of dirt should be finished with a paint used for children's furniture, which results in a smooth, washable, very durable surface; do not use oil-based paints or paints that contain lead.

You can see your birds best through a dark mesh. I like to use galvanized hardware cloth (½ inch [12 millimeters]) with the wire enclosed in dark green plastic. Nowadays, wire netting for bird cages that is made entirely of plastic (black) and tough enough to resist the bills of Zebra Finches is also available. Mesh with a chrome or brass finish reflects the light and, if the finish is rough, unnecessarily injures the ceres on your birds' bills. The finished panels of smooth galvanized mesh that you can buy in various sizes (up to 50 inches [127 centimeters] long) are better. Doors are already built in, and no frame is required. You can also buy larger mesh walls with frames. Or you can build your own frames out of lath or aluminum moldings and cover them with a netting of your choice—a process that is not simple, however.

Manufacturers of aviaries also offer clean-out drawers made of synthetic materials and in many sizes. I have used—and been very satisfied with—the indestructible pans sold for developing film. Two of these pans measuring 19 × 23 inches (47 × 57 centimeters) work very well, for instance, for a small aviary with a floor area of 20 × 48 inches (50 × 120 centimeters) and any height you like.

## The Right Location

The home of Zebra Finches is not an object that you can put here one day and there another. The birds need a permanent place and like to look down on their caretaker from above. They feel uneasy when exposed on all sides, and they are bothered by too much traffic in front of their cage, by cigarette smoke, by a too-loud radio or television, or by the ultrahigh frequencies emitted by remote control switches for television. I would not recommend putting the cage in front of a window, because in the winter the cage will be too dark and in the summer the direct sun will make it too bright and hot. Also, to be able to see your birds, you would have to use a cage that is open on all sides. If you do use such a cage, it is best to place it against a wall at about eye level. The best solution is to find a quiet, draft-free corner. If your cage does not come with a stand, I would suggest putting the cage on a piece of furniture or a shelf about 3 to 5 feet (1 to 1.5 meters) above floor level. Shelving that rests on braces fitted into vertical runners offers several advantages: You can determine the length and width of the shelves yourself and can mount the shelves at the height you like. You can also add more shelves above and below for things like lighting, accessories, and reference material. I have found this kind of setup very convenient.

## Temperature and Humidity

Zebra Finches do not need as much heat as other kinds of exotic finches. But coming originally from the steppes, they lose their relative resistance to cooler temperatures when kept in more humid climes (p. 68). You had therefore best keep your Zebra Finches at normal room temperature with a relative humidity of 50% to 70% (60% to 70% during incubation). In other words, if you feel cozy, your Zebra Finches will be comfortable, too, though they can winter over in temperatures as low as 43°F (6°C) and will even breed at 54°F (12°C).

Zebra Finches that live in an outdoor aviary or in an open-air shelter suffer when the weather is cool and wet. They should therefore be kept outdoors only from June to August. The first few days of raw weather are the most critical for them.

## Daylight and Artificial Light

Zebra Finches are happiest and raise their young most successfully if they get 12 to 14 hours of natural daylight or can be active that long with the help of artificial light. If you want to provide your Zebra Finches with an environment that resembles that natural one as much as possible, you will therefore have to resort to fluorescent lights, especially during the winter. With Vita Lite, you can achieve a good substitute for missing daylight. In calculating how much fluorescent lighting is needed, assume 40 watts per square meter. If you use Vita Lite, consult your dealer, as it comes in various models that differ in the amount of lighting furnished. All models fit into the normal sockets.

I mount the lamps on the underside of shelves about 6 inches (15 centimeters) above the aviaries, and I would recommend using at least one tube running the entire length of the aviary or a combination of two shorter ones. Many bird keepers hook up the lights to a timer that turns them on and off at the desired times. Not only is this a convenience for the keeper, but the birds appreciate a steady rhythm of light and dark that reflects the conditions of their natural habitat. It is advisable to have a dimming phase in the evening so that the birds are not surprised by the dark and thus prevented from getting back to their sleeping nests. If this happens, they flutter about in a panic and may injure themselves. And if there are eggs or fledglings in the nest, they are deprived of the warmth of the sitting bird.

Unfortunately, connecting fluorescent lamps to automatic dimmers, which are quite expensive, is complicated. But you can achieve the dimming more simply and more cheaply by hooking up a second timer that turns on an 8-watt tube or a 15-

watt bulb and later turns it off again. An even easier way is to keep a night light burning in the room (not over the aviary) all night.

## Perches for Zebra Finches

Green branches with the bark on make the best perches for Zebra Finches. Since branches are springy, of various thickness, and not as monotonously horizontal as the

A swing mounted as shown here rocks back and forth only very little, so that the birds are not frightened.

Behavior typical of Zebra Finches.  ▷
Upper left and right: The female is asking the male for a head check, and the male obliges.
Middle left: Even when upside down a Zebra Finch does not fall off a perch; Middle right: A female is scratching her head.
Lower left: Immature Zebra Finch is begging from a male; Lower right: Rubbing the head feathers against the perch after a bath.

bars in the cage, they keep the legs and toes flexible. But natural branches have to be replaced quite frequently because they dry out quickly and get hard. They are also difficult to keep clean (mites like to hide under the cracked bark).

Unsprayed branches of most bushes and trees (e.g., maple, birch, elderberry, arborvitae, fruit trees, poplar, willow) can be used, as well as the stalks of reeds, which are especially good for wearing down the birds' toenails. Obviously, you should not damage protected plants in your search for natural branches nor should you raid nature preserves.

In a small aviary you can of course use normal ⅜- or ½-inch (10- or 12-millimeter) dowels. Most of the perches should be thick enough that the Zebra Finches cannot reach all the way around them, or the toenails will not get any wear. If the perches are too thin, the birds cannot sit up straight. Large rings or swings can also be used if they do not rock too much and make the birds nervous.

Special aluminum brackets designed for holding branches can be screwed into the walls of aviaries. Bunches of reeds can be inserted through holes in two thin pieces of wood or plastic and arranged to stick up at an angle. Branches or dowels should be placed in such a way that the birds cannot simply hop from one to another but are forced to fly a small distance. I have built out of beech wood two "sitting trees" for each of my small aviaries and set them up at least 20 inches (50 centimeters) apart. These trees consist of a "trunk" made of a ⅝-inch (14- or 16-millimeter) dowel with many ⅜- or ½-inch (10- or 12-centimeter) horizontal perches, from which smaller (¼-inch [6- or 8-millimeter]) dowels can branch off. Using an electric drill, I had no problems drilling the holes for the smaller dowels. I painted these trees with a thin coat of varnish; this provides no real protection against the droppings, but the wood keeps a rough surface, does not rot, and is easier to clean.

Hollow coconuts and wickerwork nests make good sleeping nests, but to serve as brood nests they have to be quite large.

## Sleeping and Incubating Nests

Most Zebra Finches spend the night sleeping in a nest rather than on a perch. Each pair therefore needs one or two hollow coconuts or wickerwork nests in the shape of a tube or a sphere with an opening. Since the birds will sooner or later attempt to raise a family in these nests, you should buy or build nesting sites of appropriate size at the beginning.

Zebra Finches are not fussy and will gratefully accept any aid to breeding. They will make do with either the spacious nesting boxes or the large basket nests you can buy for a few dollars at a pet shop. If you decide to build nesting boxes yourself out of plywood, be sure the interior dimensions are at least 4 × 4 × 4 inches (10 × 10 × 10 centimeters). A length and a height of 5 to 6 inches (12 to 15 centimeters) are even better.

I give my Zebra Finches only semi-open nesting boxes, because if I provided them with nests that already have an entry hole and a perch there would be nothing left for

Check every day to make sure the automatic food dispenser is working properly.

them to do. Nest building is part of the natural repertoire of Zebra Finch behavior, and the birds should have a chance to engage in it. Feel free, therefore, to offer them some more open nesting sites, such as a bowl-shaped basket nest resting on a forked branch or a semicircle of wood with holes drilled diagonally along the edge into which you stich some twigs.

Since every pair needs two nests to choose from, you can provide some variety with a coconut or with a nest woven of palm leaves. Coconuts are especially easy to clean and offer hardly any hiding places for mites. But to make suitable nests they have to measure at least 4¾ inches (12 centimeters) in diameter (15 inches [38 centimeters] in circumference).

If you happen to find a large, round coconut of unusual perfection at your grocery store, with a keyhole saw make a 2-inch (4.5- to 5.5-centimeter) hole and scoop out the meat. To hang the coconut nest, use a hook made of florist's wire or a screw hook with nuts. Nesting boxes can be screwed to the wall with wing nuts.

## Food and Water Containers

I use four food containers for each aviary: a long flat dish or an automatic dispenser for the usual birdseed mixture and three smaller dishes for Mineral-A-Grit (Sunshine Birds and Supplies, Miami, FL), soft foods, and wild seeds. I also have a very shallow dish containing sprouted seeds and food for the young (rearing food) and a larger one for sand, grit, and eggshells.

# Housing and Equipment

Small, shallow containers made of light materials (shallow tin cans, jar tops, saucers for flowerpots) tend to tip over when the birds jump up on the rim. That is why I prefer to use heavy glazed pottery saucers 3 inches (8 centimeters) in diameter. (Pet stores sell a great variety of glass and porcelain dishes.) The rest of the food containers are made of synthetic materials and are attached to the wall.

Unlike other aviculturists, I have been pleased with automatic seed dispensers. Of course, some empty seed husks run through it and drop into the eating bowl, but they are "washed" to the top by the seeds that slide down with them, and the fluttering wings of the birds blow them off. A problem arises only when the bowl gets almost empty and the husks begin to collect at the top. The dispenser can clog if moisture gets into the food and causes it to get moldy or, worse yet, allows insect larvae to get established in it.

For bathing, Zebra Finches need a bathhouse of about 5 × 5 × 5 inches (13 × 13 × 13 centimeters), a standard item at pet stores, that hooks onto the side of a cage or, if you have a large enough aviary, that can be placed on the floor. If the shallow water pan is large enough, two birds can take a bath at the same time. A fancier of exotic finches I visited had large bathhouses built of 3/16-inch- (4-millimeter-) thick plexiglass and acrylic glue.

Automatic water dispensers or small water dishes make sense only if the birds are supposed to get small amounts of vitamins or medicines and if there is no bath the birds can drink from.

# Suitable Food and Proper Feeding

## Food and Feeding

Apart from accommodations, the most important factor affecting your birds' health is the kind of food you give them. Birds, like human beings, have to eat a variety of foods to stay healthy. Seed-eating birds need primarily carbohydrates and lesser amounts of fats and proteins for energy. They always have to get all the amino acids (building blocks of proteins) as well as the necessary minerals and trace elements in sufficient amounts. If a bird is deprived of any of these, it will get deficiency diseases and ultimately die. Zebra Finches are seed eaters but also feed on insects and tender leaves. The bulk of their natural diet consists of a great variety of green, ripe, and sprouting grass seeds. In captivity they receive a substitute of all kinds of millet seeds. Animal proteins are supplied through soft foods. Each kind of food contains somewhat different nutrients, and the more variety you offer, the more closely you will be duplicating the birds' natural diet and the smaller will be the chance of deficiency diseases. That is why it is important to offer a balanced mixture of seeds, whether in one large food dispenser (p. 20) or in several dishes. It is extremely important, however, that the food not be exposed to splashing bath water or droppings; otherwise, there is danger of contamination with pathogenic molds or bacteria.

Like other kinds of food, seeds have their full nutritional value only if they have not been stored too long. Check to see that the birdseed is not dusty and does not smell musty. The germination rate is the best indicator: Count out 100 seeds of one sort and place them in lukewarm water to sprout (see ''Sprouted Seeds,'' p. 24); if more than 60% sprout, that particular batch is fine.

If you buy birdseed in bulk, keep it in a dry, dark, but well-aired place. I store my seeds in large coffee cans with small holes in the covers. Mineral food and soft foods keep perfectly well in closed cans or jars.

Never cut back on your Zebra Finches' diet by limiting them to one feeding a day or by giving them only one kind of food. A good birdseed mixture provides a nutritionally complete diet. Your birds will eat their fill but will not overeat. If they should get obese, this is due solely to lack of exercise. Even a short period of fasting can do permanent damage to the health of these tiny birds.

## Seeds

Millet is essential for keeping Zebra Finches healthy. The collective term *millet* refers to a number of different wild and cultivated grasses that are easy to grow and are usually imported from the warmer countries of the world. Millet is consequently available all year.

As a Zebra Finch fancier you should be able to recognize the most important kinds of millet. The light yellowish Senegal and Mohair millets and the orange-to-corn-colored Manna millet are quite small grained. Among the larger-grained varieties are the brownish gray Japan millet, the oval yellowish La Plata millet (yellow millet), silver or white millet, the reddish brown Mo-

# Suitable Food and Proper Feeding

Sprouts should be served in a very shallow dish.

rocco millet (golden millet), and the red Dakota millet (red millet). Zebra Finches eat them all happily, though they are a little less enthusiastic about the last two on the list. The names under which the various kinds of millet are sold are not always totally correct, because often there is no one-to-one match between the botanical designations and the names customarily used by farmers and dealers. Nor do the names necessarily reflect where the millet actually comes from. A very good Senegal millet, for instance, is grown in Australia.

A great delicacy among almost all exotic finches is spray millet, which is raised primarily in America, France, Italy, and China. The birds probably like it so much because the seed stays fresher and tastes better. Do not buy this millet by the spray but by weight instead. Check the quality and compare prices. Cardboard boxes giving no indication of weight and containing only three or four sprays are outrageously expensive, and their contents are often hidden from view for good reason. One- or two-pound bags are usually quite a good buy. Some varieties of millet do well in our temperate zones. They can be planted in a garden and either fed green or frozen at that stage.

Canary or White seed is just as good for birds as millet. Some Zebra Finches also like oat germ. But millet, canary, and oats contain over 50% carbohydrates and are thus relatively low in proteins and fats; they are therefore counted among the starchy seeds. Oily seeds, such as rapeseed, niger, lettuce seed, linseed, and poppy seed, have a much higher proportion of fats and proteins. Niger especially should be added only in small quantities; these seeds are long and thin and look just like lettuce seeds except for being pitch black.

The standard fare I put in the food dispenser consists of a mixture of one third small-grained millet (Senegal and Manna) and two thirds of a combination of La Plata, silver, and Japan millet and canary with a small addition of niger. Some aviculturists offer the niger separately in a small dish instead.

If you prefer not to or cannot buy the different kinds of seeds individually at a seed store or a pet store, you can use a

You can offer these grasses to your Zebra Finches: annual bluegrass, Italian rye grass, red fescue, and meadow fescue (from left to right).

23

packaged mixture designed for exotic finches. A good firm lists on the package the mixture contents and date of packing. Seed should not be more than one year old.

You can also buy lettuce, clover, poppy, and various other seeds, but these should be fed only in small amounts. I always give my birds a separate dish of a commercial mixture of wild seeds as well.

## Sprouted Seeds

I have already mentioned that Zebra Finches like to eat some greens and ripening grasses, which they are especially fond of because immature seeds have a high moisture content and are therefore high in vitamins and easily digestible. Sprouted seeds are a good substitute. In the process of swelling up and sprouting, seeds produce vitamins and other nutrients that are especially crucial for the rearing of baby birds. Since the growing sprouts gradually deplete the food value of the grain, it is best to feed the sprouted seeds when they have just started germinating. Sprouts should be served on very flat dishes so that air can circulate freely through them. All the millet varieties mentioned can be used for sprouting in a mixture because they germinate at about the same time. Seed mixtures with added nutrients ("protein pellets") are not so suitable.

The following methods of sprouting have shown good results because they prevent souring and mold:

• Soak the seeds in lukewarm water for 12 hours, then rinse in a sieve and let germinate another 24 hours in a covered bowl (moist but without water). If the seeds are covered with water, the sprouts cannot develop, because they drown.

• Sprout makers, commercially available in larger and smaller sizes (for our purpose, the smaller are better), work very well. They consist of four sprouting dishes stacked one above the other, with a dish to catch the runoff at the bottom. The water runs through the four perforated dishes, cleaning and moistening the seeds that have been spread into small rills. But you have to check on the sprouts, because small seeds can plug up the system.

## Greens and Fruit

Even more nutritionally valuable than sprouts are the many local grasses and weeds of which Zebra Finches eat not only the fruit but often the leaves and stems as well. The reason these plants are not utilized more is that most of us are ignorant about the flora in our own backyards. Fewer and fewer people know their native plant world, and many species of wild plants are becoming extinct. I was just as ignorant as the next person. When I came across an old biology textbook from my school days, I realized just how much I had forgotten.

Now there are available many excellent illustrated guides to plant identification that can help bird keepers get to know the many plants that can be used as bird food. There are native millets that can be grown in your garden, as well as many other

# Suitable Food and Proper Feeding

Chickweed, *Bellis perennis* (European), dandelions, and shepherd's purse (from left to right) are plants that birds like to eat and that are easy to find.

grasses, such as English and Italian rye grass; sheep, meadow, and red fescue; orchard grass; quack grass; brome grass; annual bluegrass; and other bluegrasses. Annual bluegrass (*Poa annua*), one of a number of grass species that were introduced into Australia by Europeans, has become one of the main food sources for Zebra Finches there. By the way, rushes and sedges are marsh plants, some of which are protected and therefore should not be harvested for feeding your birds.

Other plants birds sometimes like to eat are more common: chickweed, dandelion, English and common plantain, forget-me-not, shepherd's purse, tansy ragwort, cuckoo flower, yarrow, curled dock, pale smartweed, bull thistle, and sow thistle. You will have to proceed by trial and error to see just what appeals to your birds. One plant you can be sure will be popular is the appropriately named chickweed. If you give it good soil and keep it moist, you can even winter over chickweed in a light but not too warm spot indoors.

In most cases, the birds are interested not in the plant's leaves but in its maturing or ripe seeds, which should always be given on the stem. Pick dandelion before the fluffy white seed balls are fully developed. Cut them with scissors so that the ripe seeds, which are connected by fine stems to downy tufts (the pappi), will not go floating through the aviary and entire room.

Another depressing but perfectly good reason that many bird keepers prefer not to collect indigenous plants for their birds is the poisoning of our environment. Herbicides and pesticides, overfertilization of agricultural land, and progressive air pollution can poison forage plants. This presents a threat to Zebra Finches that is becoming more and more likely. Only in areas free of these pressures can we still find places to safely gather plants to feed our birds.

That is why I usually make do with a commercial mixture of wild seeds supplemented with chickweed, dandelion, lettuce (including corn salad and chicory), parsley, fruit, slices of cucumber, and grated carrot. Add to this a potted plant—the easy-to-keep and fast-growing *Tradescantia viridis* (of the spiderwort family), which, with its green leaves, is not particularly attractive and is therefore considered practically a weed in many plant nurseries. Be sure to at least try apples, bananas, grapes, and other fruit on your birds. In time you will find all kinds of foods your Zebra Finches like. Taste varies with the individual bird, and

Different color variants of Zebra Finches.
Upper left: Cream (hen on the left, cock on the right);
Upper right: Dominant Silver (cock).
Middle left: Penguin Gray (hen on the left, cock on

the right); Middle right: Crested Dominant Silver (hen). ▷
Lower left: Black-breasted Gray (hen on the left, cock
on the right); Lower right: Black-breasted Pied, gray
with yellow bill (hen).

Chickweed is as popular among Zebra Finches as among other birds. It grows along meadows and roads, in gardens, and even on barren soil. If you transplant it in the spring, it will even thrive in a window box.

anything new will at first be regarded with suspicion.

Greens, whether bought at a store or gathered in the wild, have to be washed and dried or let drip thoroughly before being fed. It should go without saying that bird lovers will not use poisons in their own gardens.

## Soft and Rearing Foods

Zebra Finches need protein from animal sources only for raising their young, and even then the nestlings need less animal proteins than do the offspring of most other exotic finches. Too much protein can have dangerous consequences if it leaves the digestive system of young birds unable to adapt to the customary adult diet of seeds.

Your birds' vegetarian tastes make life a lot easier for you. There is no need to raise, catch, or buy mealworms, ant pupae, flies, larvae, or daphnia; instead you can simply use a commercially available, non-souring rearing food or special preparations designed for insect eaters or soft-billed birds. Rearing food consists of crumbs, egg, insects, wild seeds, minerals, and vitamins.

When my Zebra Finches have babies, I mix rearing food with some cooked egg (especially the yolk), low-fat cottage cheese, or finely grated carrot. I prepare this mixture fresh every day because it dries out and spoils quickly. The birds always look forward eagerly to a meal of this homemade concoction, especially to the egg version. Cooked egg shells provide a very popular source of minerals.

## Minerals and Trace Elements

If Zebra Finches are given a good, well-balanced diet, they get adequate amounts of the important trace elements and vitamins. But additional minerals, especially calcium and phosphorus, have to be provided. Calcium, together with vitamin D, is needed, for instance, for the formation of the skeleton and of eggshells. The cannibalistic craving for eggshells of many laying hens shows this.

Cuttlebone, the shells of chicken eggs, liquid calcium supplements to be added to the drinking water, bird grit, and special mineral preparations are all good sources of calcium. My birds all like Mineral-A-Grit, which also contains trace elements and vitamins and can be either mixed into the soft food or given separately in a small dish.

A product such as Ornalyte (Mardel) com-

◁ Cultivated strains of the Timor Zebra Finch.
Upper left: Masked white (cock on the left, hen on the right); Upper right: naturally colored Timor Zebra Finches (*Taeniopygia guttata guttata*, hen on the left, cock on the right).

Middle left: White (cock); Middle right: Gray Ticked (cock).
Lower left: Gray Back (cock); Lower right: Pied Gray (cock).

bines electrolytes and trace minerals, fortified with high-potency vitamin complex.

A cheap source of calcium is pulverized plaster of paris. You can sprinkle some regularly on the floor of the cage or put it in a bowl. Forest soil is also rich in minerals.

## Vitamins

Small but regular amounts of vitamin supplements should be given to make up for a diet that may be too one-sided or may contain too small a variety of dry seeds. Vitamin supplements also help offset the lack of natural sunshine. This is necessary because the plants or seeds that birds eat often contain vitamins only in a preliminary stage, "previtamins" that are transformed into real vitamins only with the help of ultraviolet rays. Many manufacturers sell "finished" or complete vitamins either individually for special needs or in a combination of several vitamins. These latter multivitamins include the most important water-soluble vitamins (B, C) as well as the fat-soluble ones (A, D, E, K). By using such a multivitamin you give your birds all the necessary vitamins in a balanced combination and thus avoid one-sided or excessive dosages. Be sure not to neglect giving vitamins because:

The *A vitamins* are essential for development of the embryo and for the health of the eyes, plumage, mucous membranes, and the respiratory, digestive, and reproductive systems.

The *D vitamins* prevent rickets and egg

Zebra Finches like to eat immature grass seeds that they cleverly pick out from the seed heads.

binding, because they aid the building of bones and eggshells from calcium and phosphorus.

The need for vitamins A and D can be covered with the "finished" vitamins (i.e., supplements), but be sure not to supply them in excess!

*Vitamin E* plays an important role in metabolism and fertility and is therefore crucial for successful breeding.

*Vitamin K* regulates the clotting of blood.

*Vitamins of the B complex* are especially important for metabolism, growth, and the nervous system. B vitamins have to be supplied in artificial form whenever a bird gets medications (antibiotics) that destroy intestinal flora and thus inhibit the production of these vitamins. (A vitamin supplement with a high proportion of B vitamins may smell a little.)

29

# Suitable Food and Proper Feeding

*Vitamin C* is also produced by the bird's body. It is involved in the metabolism of cells and protects against infections but does not seem to be as important for birds as it is for human beings.

Vitamins are needed in minute but regular amounts, because birds need them continually but are unable to store them. The supplements are available in liquid (dissolved in an emulsion) or powdered form. They can be added to either the drinking water or the food. If they are dissolved in water, however, they stay fresh for only a short time. In addition, Zebra Finches may be put off by the color or smell of the vitamin-enriched water and may refuse even to try it. That is why I use vitamins exclusively in powdered form, sprinkling them in tiny amounts on rearing food or sprouts. Vitamins, by the way, are extremely sensitive to heat, light, and oxygen.

The water in drinking dishes and bathing bowls should never be deeper than ¾ of an inch (2 centimeters). It is best to place a stone in the middle of the bowl; this way young birds will find a good footing when they land.

## Sand and Water

Birds do not have teeth to chew their food, and Zebra Finches are no exception. As seed eaters, they grind up food in their muscular gizzards with the aid of grains of sand and little pebbles. That is the reason you have to provide some not-too-fine sand in a dish or sprinkle it over the floor of the cage. Bird grit is just as good if in addition to sand kernels it contains some crushed seashell (i.e., calcium). Digestion is also stimulated by charcoal, which Zebra Finches consume in their natural habitat as well. A thin layer of sand facilitates the weekly cleaning of the floor of the aviary,

because the droppings can be swept up more easily with the sand.

Except during the reproductive cycle, Zebra Finches are less dependent on water than are many other kinds of birds, but they do bathe and drink water regularly. They should always have clear, unchlorinated, and not-too-cold water at their disposal.

Tap water can be improved with a liquid additive such as Ornacycline (Mardel), Vitaflight (Mardel), or Avimin (Lambert Kay). You can also use regular mineral water. Carbonic acid (or the chlorine in tap water) can be removed by boiling the water or letting it stand. I use a household filter (ion exchanger) that filters out not only calcium (which you may be familiar with in the form of deposits in teakettles) but also chlorine, heavy metals, and organic pollutants.

Dirty water is very dangerous for birds, and you therefore have no choice but to clean the bath every day and replenish it with ¾ inch (2 centimeters) of fresh water.

# The Keeping and Care of Zebra Finches

## The Trip Home and Acclimation

The pet dealer will probably hand your Zebra Finches to you in the kind of cardboard box generally used for small birds. Place this box with the air holes up in a small bag to protect the birds against the elements. Then get home with them as quickly as possible. There everything should be ready for them. After all, your new charges will have to find their way around in an entirely new environment, and after the shock of having been caught and transported they should not have to be further frightened by any avoidable fuss and handling. What is crucial is that the birds find their accustomed food right away. So, for this once, sprinkle some food on the floor or hang some of the popular millet sprays in the cage before the newcomers' arrival.

Once the birds have been settled in their cage they need peace and quiet. Watch them from a distance. Perhaps they will flutter about wildly at first, but eventually they will calm down and start eating. They have to familiarize themselves with their new home and take possession of it before they feel safe and secure.

If you want to introduce a single bird or a pair into an aviary that already has birds living in it, a one-week quarantine in a smaller cage is recommended. It is true that acclimation is delayed this way, but you have a better chance to observe the new birds and, if there are any signs of illness, to treat the birds.

The initial agitation subsides quickly when a Zebra Finch discovers the reassuring presence of another member of its species or, better yet, of a familiar partner purchased at the same time. Soon the two will be perching wing to wing.

It is not easy to get Zebra Finches used to a cover over their cage. Leave a small bulb burning at least during the first few nights. Zebra Finches are more easily frightened than canaries and could hurt themselves seriously by panicked thrashing around in the dark.

Check to make sure your birds have found and are eating the birdseed you have supplied. There is no need to feed them other kinds of food right away. In fact, soft foods and greens might damage the linings of the stomach and intestines if these are weakened by a change in food and the adjustment to a new place.

But there is no need to feel overly anxious about Zebra Finches; they are surprisingly robust and resilient. If the birds you bought are healthy and if you house them and care for them properly, they will survive the acclimating phase without problems. Still, it is advisable during the first days and weeks to keep an especially vigilant eye on the birds' state of health, which includes constant and careful examination of the droppings (p. 57). At this stage the only preventive measures against illness are warmth, fresh air (but no drafts!), and quiet. You should wait before you start giving your birds a suitable vitamin combination, and you should never give them antibiotics as a preventive measure (see "A Medicine Cabinet for Birds," p. 57).

If you are careful not to scare your Zebra Finches with hasty movements, they will quickly get used to you as their new caretaker and to their new surroundings. Now

31

you can experiment to see which kinds of food appeal to them the most and let them fly around the room while you clean their cage. Zebra Finches need a lot of time to familiarize themselves with their surroundings before they can find their way back to their cage. And remember that flying free always involves dangers—even a closed window can be fatal if it is not protected by a curtain (see "List of Dangers," p. 34). You will be able to tell when you let your Zebra Finches fly free (if not before) whether they are good flyers. Sometimes, newly purchased birds at first plummet to the ground while fluttering frantically with their wings, because they were raised in a small cage where all they could do was hop around. If these birds are young, their flight muscles will improve rapidly in an aviary.

Introducing a new bird into an aviary with an already established population may present a problem, because the old timers may gang up against it. This behavior is not at all unnatural. But if the newcomer is allowed to establish sight and sound contact with its fellows for a few days from a nearby cage or a separate section of the aviary, the established birds will have a chance to get to know and accept their new neighbor. The acclimation works even better if the new bird is at first introduced to just the one bird intended to become its partner.

## Chores

Zebra Finches kept in captivity are not able to build up as much immunity against all kinds of pathogens as their fellows in the wild do. In addition, the more crowded conditions in an aviary allow poisonous substances to accumulate faster and in greater concentrations than in nature, where all kinds of pollution are cleared up more quickly.

The unnatural living conditions prevailing in aviaries therefore force bird owners to perform a continuing round of cleaning chores. The rule formulated by aquarists also holds for aviculturists—namely, the smaller the living space, the larger the amount of work. And for the keeper of Zebra Finches, work means:

• *Daily*
Clean dirty food dishes; check food hoppers or refill dishes; provide fresh sprouts and/or fresh food; prepare rearing food if necessary; clean and refill water dish; supply nesting materials; observe birds and remove any you suspect of being ill.

• *Weekly*
Thoroughly clean all dirty parts of the aviary; wash branches, perches, and rocks; replenish sand; hoe the soil.

• *Monthly*
Everything must be cleaned. Clean out the nest; replace branches; disinfect cages with mites; check aviaries—especially outdoor ones—for rust, rotting, and weak spots; make necessary repairs; make major changes in the aviary; clip the birds' toenails if necessary.

The monthly chores often require that the

birds leave the cage and fly free. These chores should be performed in the morning so that the birds will have plenty of time when they return to their cage to readjust to the perhaps somewhat changed looks of their home and to find new sleeping or nesting sites if the old ones have been removed. If your Zebra Finches are in the process of raising a family, it is better to take care of only the most pressing matters and to postpone the cleaning of the cage and the nesting box until a week after the fledglings have left the nest.

Use only hot water to clean the cage and accessories; cleansers and rinses can be extremely hazardous to your charges.

## Dangers for Your Zebra Finches

Pet birds live dangerously—both in and out of their cages. In the "List of Dangers" on page 34 I first mention dangers lurking inside the cage, dangers that are perhaps easier to avoid than the risks inherent in free flying (enumerated in the second part of the list).

Birds are obviously not programmed by nature to exist in human environments (i.e., our living rooms), and when they are outside their aviary, our technological gadgets (electric outlets, toasters, etc.) can easily spell disaster for them. I would therefore recommend that you keep your Zebra Finches' free-flying time to a minimum and compensate for this by keeping them in a large enough aviary so that they have no need for free flying.

Next to infections of the respiratory and the digestive organs, escape is the main cause for loss of Zebra Finches. I found out myself one day just how dangerous relaxed vigilance can be. I had accidentally left the door of the cage open, and one of my male Zebra Finches (Matz), together with his mate, flew through the hallway into a room with an open window. The pair immediately settled on a low, enameled parapet right outside the window, apparently thinking they were still separated from the outside by glass. At first I was paralyzed with horror, picturing how they might slide off the smooth ledge or simply fly away. Luckily I was able to shoo them back into the room with a broom. If it had not been for this stroke of genius on my part, the birds would have escaped and would no doubt soon have died of hunger or a cold or met with some other disaster.

Dangers of free flying: If a Zebra Finch collides with a window, the injuries are generally fatal.

## List of Dangers

| Source of Danger | Effects |
|---|---|
| Drafts from airing the house; open windows and doors | Colds |
| Damp, cool air; cold | Colds; freezing |
| Direct sunlight; overheated rooms | Heat stroke; heart failure |
| Spoiled or dirty food; chlorinated or polluted water | Intestinal disorders; infections |
| Wrong type of food | Intestinal disorders; deficiency diseases |
| Bath water over ¾ inch (2 centimeters) deep | Drowning (especially fledglings) |
| Unsuitable nesting material; cage decorations, cubbyholes, and other traps; overgrown claws | Getting caught: broken bones or surface wounds |
| Too many perches | Fractures |
| Sharp edges on wire mesh, wire ends, nails | Toe and head injuries |
| Mesh with opening wider than ½ inch (12 millimeters) | Sticking head through mesh: getting stuck or strangling |
| Total darkness; mites | Frenzied fluttering at night: broken bones or surface wounds |
| Varnishes; sprays for dry cleaning, personal hygiene, or bugs; traces of cleansers and chemicals | Poisoning |
| Open cage doors; holes in aviary mesh | Escape |
| Open windows and doors | Flying away |
| Window panes without curtains | Flying against the glass with possibly fatal results |
| Spaces between walls and furniture | Getting stuck |
| Open drawers and cabinets | Getting locked in and suffocating |
| Open containers with cold or hot liquids (toilet, sinks, vases, pots, serving dishes) | Drowning, getting burned |
| Kitchen vapors | Internal illnesses |
| Cook stoves, toasters, heating stoves, fireplaces | Burns |
| Electrical outlets; exposed wires | Electrical shock |
| Threads, yarns; knitted or crocheted articles | Getting entangled and strangling |
| Other pets (cats, dogs, rabbits) | Getting killed |
| Inattentive people | Getting sat on or stepped on |

# The Keeping and Care of Zebra Finches

## Handling Zebra Finches

Animals need to keep at a certain distance from members of their own species as well as from other creatures, and especially from enemies. If their safety zone is invaded, they react with either aggression or flight.

In the case of Zebra Finches, early individual experience (contact with humans from birth) has had the effect of lessening this individual distance toward their caretakers, so that we can watch them from quite close without interfering in their normal business of eating, bathing, or raising young. Still, Zebra Finches are clearly more nervous than canaries and will attempt to get away when we do anything right next to or above their cages. Since flight is out of the question in a cage no more than 16 inches (40 centimeters) deep, Zebra Finches panic in such a situation. So take your birds' need for a safety zone into consideration. Approach the aviary slowly at first. When they show signs of nervousness, you have reached the outer limit of their individual distance. You will notice that this distance grows less every day. Avoid all hasty or abrupt movements, do not come bursting into the room suddenly, and do not choose a spot near the aviary to shake out a tablecloth.

If you have a sufficiently large aviary, you are at a great advantage. There, in their very own realm, the birds feel much more secure than anywhere else in the room, and they will stay calm and relaxed even when you replace food and clean up.

My own birds demonstrated this very clearly. When they lived in a small cage, it was always a nerve-wracking enterprise to get them back in, and when hunger finally forced them to return, I had to snap the gate shut behind them instantly. Now it is difficult to lure them out of the aviary at all.

Occasions will arise when you have no choice but to catch one of your birds. When this happens you should proceed as gently and as quickly as you can. Do not attempt to catch a bird in a small aviary; after all, that is the place where a bird is supposed to feel secure and at ease. The place to catch a bird is in a room or in a room-sized aviary.

If you are quick, you maybe able to use your hand to grab the bird. First, turn the light off as soon as the bird has settled down somewhere, and then catch it; your eyesight will be better in the dark than the bird's. If this method does not appeal to you, use a bird net with a soft frame, available at pet stores. Never try to catch a bird in flight by whipping the net over it; you might hit the bird with the wire part and break a wing. The easiest way to net a Zebra Finch is when it is sitting down or flying slowly and cautiously in dim light.

Catch your Zebra Finches only when absolutely necessary. These tiny birds often go into shock when they are caught and then lie in your hand as though dead. My Zebra Finch Matz has not been able to get over this "ordeal of terror" to this day.

# The Keeping and Care of Zebra Finches

## How Zebra Finches Spend Their Days

Let us assume you bought one pair or three pairs of Zebra Finches a few days ago and want to spend your first full day at home getting to know your little friends. (By the way: I state three pairs instead of two for a specific reason: Two pairs mean "war," as the males will compete for dominance. By keeping three or more pairs in a cage or aviary, all will be peaceful.)

The first thing you will notice is that Zebra Finches are not late sleepers. The moment there is light, they are wide awake and ready to greet the morning with a loud concert. First you will hear loud, drawn-out notes; then, the typical song of the males. But the excitement soon subsides, giving way to busy stretching of wings and legs and whetting of beaks. Next the birds eat breakfast, have a sip of water, and, later in the morning, bathe.

When you place a dish of sprouts or fresh food in the aviary, the birds crane their necks forward and peer down curiously first with one eye and then with the other. This twisting of the head from side to side is necessary, because the eyes of Zebra Finches are placed on the side of the head.

After the bath it is time for a thorough preening of the plumage. The birds stretch out their wings to draw the feathers on the inside of the wing through the beak one by one. Then they sit up straight and groom the spread-out belly feathers. Finally, with the tail raised high, they take care of the feathers on the rump and sides and the tail coverts and tail feathers.

In between, the birds keep scratching their heads, necks, and throats. This happens at such speed that at first you hardly notice it. Zebra Finches also like to have these places groomed by their partners, squatting down on a perch or on the ground for these ministrations and even shutting their eyes.

The plumage is groomed every day meticulously and at length.

You can easily tell whether two birds have taken a liking to each other. If they have, they will be found sitting together un-usually often, pecking shyly at each other's feathers at first. Soon thereafter, they will engage in almost all activities together and

# The Keeping and Care of Zebra Finches

even coordinate many of their movements and postures.

This tendency to stimulate communal activities is typical of these sociable birds in general. If one bird decides to have a bath, it will not be long before a whole row of them will be sitting on a perch with dripping feathers and shaking off the water. And when after a period of activity one Zebra Finch begins to doze, the whole lot will be asleep in no time, sometimes with their heads turned to the back.

The birds' noisy doings will be broken up by a number of these naps in the course of a day. These are the only times when you do not hear the constant "det . . . det" with which Zebra Finches maintain vocal contact with each other. It is not the Zebra Finches' song that endears them to people; in fact, many find the distinctive "trumpeting" the birds produce monotonous or even annoying. But the voices of a small Zebra Finch community are so individually varied that you will soon be able to tell each member just by listening. There are also comparable differences in behavior. Each bird has its own unmistakable personality.

It will not take long for you to get to know your "crew" and their habits very well. But to understand the birds properly, you have to know the typical behavior of Zebra Finches: what sounds they make and when, how much they eat, what they consider delicacies, and how they spend their days. So watch your birds carefully until they settle for the night in their nests. It is instructive and useful, not only for you but also for your children.

## Zebra Finches and Other Birds

Most fanciers of exotic finches who now keep and breed the most difficult and demanding species in their aviaries probably started at some point with Zebra Finches. These birds are ideal for beginners and allow you to engage in a hobby without having to worry about discouraging, fatal mistakes.

Perhaps you too will be infected by ambition or so charmed by the gorgeous colors of other kinds of birds that you will want to add variety to your aviary. Once you have gained sufficient experience with Zebra Finches there is no reason you should not branch out to just about any other kind of exotic finch as long as you know what its special requirements are.

If you decide to keep Zebra Finches together with other birds, you should restrict yourself to *Estrildidae*-species of comparable robustness and similar requirements. Your best bets would be the less-demanding species of grass finches (broadbilled *Estrildidae*), such as the Star Finch, the Long-tailed Finch, the Pictorella Finch, the Chestnut-breasted Finch, the Yellow-rumped Finch, or even the feisty Diamond Finch—all from Australia. Asian Munias—including the Spotted Munia and the White-rumped Munia, as well as its domesticated cousin, the Society Finch or Bengalese—are also recommended. The easy-to-keep African Silverbill comes, as its name implies, from Africa.

The thin-billed Waxbills from Africa are generally somewhat too delicate to coexist with Zebra Finches.

Australia, in particular, has enacted legislation that forbids the export of animals. If you want to contribute to maintaining or increasing populations in captivity of species such as the Star Finch, the Double-barred Finch, the Crimson Finch, and the Painted Finch by breeding them, you need aviaries that are considerably larger than those required for Zebra Finches.

Zebra Finches groom each other's plumage, especially on those parts of the body a bird cannot get at itself.

Canaries can also be kept together with Zebra Finches, but it will take the latter a little time to get used to the extensive flights of the canaries. At first, pandemonium broke out in my aviaries whenever our yellow canary happened to land on an aviary in the course of flying about the room. By now nobody pays much attention to it. On the other hand, I would not recommend budgerigars as companions for Zebra Finches.

# Reproduction and Breeding

## Things to Consider Before You Decide to Breed Your Birds

Raising Zebra Finches is relatively easy. If you let nature take its course, your birds will soon be ready to mate and raise a brood. But you should let them proceed only if you can create conditions that ensure success and are likely to produce healthy offspring. This requires:

• More time spent by you on your birds. In the early stages you have to prepare rearing food for the nestlings every day (p. 43), and later there will be more cleaning up to do.

• A quiet, bright, and warm place. Quiet is especially important during the incubating period, because Zebra Finches react badly to frequent disturbances at this time. The eggs are likely to hatch only if the temperature is at least 59°F (15°C) and if there are at least 12 hours of adequate light (p. 15).

• A large-enough flight cage (p. 9). If there is not enough room for the pair to go through its display ritual, no mating may take place at all. And if the young hatch successfully, you will have to accommodate not only the two parent birds in the cage but also up to five young birds that will have their first flying lessons there.

• A second cage. The young birds will need this refuge when the parents start harassing them constantly (p. 48).

• A good pair of breeders. Buy only strong, large birds of good build if you intend to breed them. Small birds or birds with defects in type (p. 8) are likely to pass these undesirable traits on to their offspring.

• Excellent care and conditions so that the breeding birds are in top health and spirits. The vigor of the young birds depends above all on the condition of the mother bird; she is the sole source of the food the developing embryos depend on as they grow inside the eggs.

• Takers for the young birds when they have developed their full coloration. After all, you will probably not be able to keep most of them yourself. Many pet stores are willing to buy the offspring of birds from their clients.

The first brood of young *Estrildidae*-species is always the most critical one, because the parent birds may not be fully mature physically and because they lack experience. Make sure your birds are at least ten months old before you let them breed. Females that are too young are more likely to suffer from egg binding (p. 60), or they may not know what to do with the eggs or the hatchlings. Older birds hardly ever have these problems.

If you do not know how old your newly purchased birds are, you should, to be on the safe side, wait three months before allowing the impatient pair to raise a family. The waiting may be as trying for you as it is for the birds, but my experience with premature broods has been uniformly bad. My Zebra Finch hen Happy, for instance, laid her first two eggs in a small sleeping nest and promptly knocked the baby birds out of it as soon as they hatched. Later on, she never did anything like this again.

There are other reasons for delaying first broods: It gives the pair a chance to get better acclimated to the aviary and to become accustomed to the caretaker; and a longer period on an especially nutritious diet results in top physical condition for the birds and, therefore, healthy offspring.

If you have a large aviary, you can have a community of birds. Zebra Finches live in flocks and breed in colonies; they do not establish territories in the sense that other birds do. But they do vigorously defend their nests and the areas immediately around them. Such a nest area is about as large as a small box cage (29 × 14 × 22 inches [74 × 36 × 56 centimeters]). Consequently, there will be major conflicts if you attempt to keep more than one pair in a small aviary. And since the birds have no chance to get out of each other's way, the fights will be fought with great venom and can even end in death.

Thus, a box-type cage of the dimensions given on page 10 will do for one pair only If you have three pairs of birds, you need an aviary at least 5 feet (1.5 meters) long and wide; an extra night shelter is also advisable.

## Selecting a Partner

Matching a pair of Zebra Finches presents no problems. Cocks and hens can easily be told apart by the color of their plumage and of their bills, and most Zebra Finches are not as fussy about choosing a partner as are other kinds of *Estrildidae*-species. If you buy a pair of birds, the two will in most cases take a liking to each other, and mate.

Of course there are exceptions. Our Matz never quite hit it off with his first (white) mate and was finally forced to raise the

Mating does not take place until an entire courtship ritual, including display songs and specific display gestures, has been performed.

brood by himself. The reason for this incompatibility may have been that White Zebra Finches differ somewhat in behavior from colored Zebra Finches (p. 73). After the sudden death of this white hen, Matz was given a new mate, this time a gray female. But the two fought with an animosity I would have thought impossible between two birds of opposite sex, and they had to be separated.

The behavior of the female gives the best clue as to how well a pair is getting along. If she likes the male, who will court her with continuous song and display rituals, she will turn her tail toward him, keep bowing, and frequently scratch his head and neck gently.

If you can and want to let your birds follow their own inclinations, you should let them pick their own partners in a group of four or more birds. If, however, your intent is to breed systematically and achieve goals you have set yourself, then you sometimes have to go counter to your Zebra Finches' leanings and keep them strictly in pairs.

Nevertheless, it is possible that two birds

absolutely do not seem suited to each other. This can be determined if they keep starting to build new nests or lay an enormously large clutch of eggs that after a few days is covered over with a new nest. In such cases the problem is best solved by separating the birds and permitting them to pair with different mates. Also, birds from premature breeding do not make good breeding couples. I have obtained the best results with one- to four-year-olds. Birds that are too old, particularly females, are also less suited for breeding. It stands to reason that intrinsically healthy offspring come from intrinsically healthy parents.

Many breeders make the common mistake of starting breeding too early. This pertains not only to Zebra Finches, but to all cage or aviary birds that regularly tend to mate too soon. Zebra Finches should be restrained; otherwise it is possible that in the dead of winter they will be sitting on eggs in their nests and expecting the babies during the most barren season of the year. Early breeding can cause the females to lose much of their strength, which affects future broods negatively. Young birds from early matings are generally not too strong, which fact becomes apparent when you wish to breed them after eight months.

Begin breeding at the end of March or the beginning of April with couples that you have kept apart during the winter months—segregating the males with other males and the females with other females (from the bands you can determine the sex). You can anticipate three to four broods that, with good care, should be striking for their purity.

## Nests and Nesting Materials

If your Zebra Finches have had only small sleeping nests up to this point, you now have to provide them with larger nesting sites so that the nestlings will not crowd each other too much later on. Always supply at least two nesting sites per pair (p. 20).

Nests should hang as high up as possible, and their openings should face the center of the aviary so that the birds will not feel watched. If you have two pairs of birds, their nests have to be located as far apart as possible in the upper corners, and the boundaries of the nest territories should be marked clearly in the center of the aviary. A "sitting tree" (p. 19) can serve as such a boundary, which will then be regarded as a neutral zone by both sets of birds, or two sitting trees can be set up with a partition between them.

Zebra Finches refuse to breed in bare hollows. They want a soft nest that they generally build out of stalks of grass. But they are not fussy and will accept nesting materials sold at pet stores, such as coconut fi-

Wooden nesting boxes for Zebra Finches that you can either buy or build yourself out of plywood (⅜- or ½-inch [8- or 12-millimeters] thick).

ber and sisal. Coconut fiber is very thin, rigid, and tough. It is therefore especially suitable for giving stability to large nests built from scratch, nests that are then padded on the inside with other, softer materials.

When you buy coconut fiber, get only the smooth combed kind, not tangled balls. Birds can easily get their feet caught in snarled coconut fibers, hemp, or any threads that are too long. My Zebra Finches like jute cord best, the kind used for macrame. I buy the biggest-size skein in natural color that I can find and then cut it into 4-inch (10-centimeter) pieces, which I then separate into the 4 to 9 individual strands they are made up of. The mother birds then break the strands down even more before incorporating them into the hollow of the nest. To start with, I place the nesting material on the bottom of the aviary, because the male bird uses up great amounts of it at first. Later on I let him pick threads out of a small food rack mounted on the outside of the cage grating, where no droppings can fall on them.

## Building the Nest

Before the cock can start building a nest, he has to make sure his mate approves of the site. Together with her, he begins by inspecting all the possible sites within the aviary. Then he tries to lure her with soft calls to join him in a nesting box. If you listen carefully you will hear soft peckings and trippings of feet from the inside of the box—there is not enough room inside for the usual hopping gait of the birds. In the

At nest-building time you have to give your Zebra Finches plenty of nesting material.

course of this inspection you will also hear a soft, drawn-out moaning sound. This does not mean that the pair is mating; rather the sound is produced by the cock in an effort to win the hen's approval of the site.

If the female gives him the go-ahead, the male can then build the nest very fast. I have watched my cinnamon-colored male Zebra Finch work furiously assembling piles of nesting material and constructing a rough nest in no more than half an hour. His enthusiasm was so great that even his mate Juppi was affected by it and helped carry some threads. Normally, however, females take part only in the actual building.

Once there is enough material in the nest you can often observe a female sticking her head out to pull in threads or stalks that

42

are hanging down messily. If the box or the coconut is large enough, Zebra Finches frequently elaborate on the basic hollow by adding walls, a roof, and even an entry tunnel. Matz, my most talented builder, always does this as a matter of course.

If you spend enough time watching your Zebra Finches during this nest-building period and if the aviary is large enough, you may be able to witness their display rituals and the mating (p. 72).

## Egg Laying and Incubation

As soon as the nest is finished—and sometimes before it is quite finished—the female starts laying her eggs. She produces one egg a day until there is a clutch of four to six eggs. Five is the most common number, but with a very young female there may be only two or three eggs. At the same time the behavior of the parents changes. Whereas the two were almost always together either inside the nest or outside during the building, there is now only one bird sitting on the eggs at all times. Male and female alternate sitting, spelling each other about every one and a half hours. The female generally spends a little more time in the nest than her partner. At night, they usually both sleep in the nest.

Normally, the behavior of the birds makes it quite clear whether there are eggs in the nest. If the pair have a nesting box with a roof that can be flipped open or slid to one side, you can check on the size of the clutch at a moment when neither bird is sitting. If you can manage to shut the parent birds into the other half of the aviary by means of a sliding partition, their agitation can be kept within bounds and they usually return to their eggs and continue brooding without problems. But such a check is really not necessary. And in the case of a young, inexperienced pair you should refrain from any kind of interference.

So be patient and wait. Usually the birds will start sitting steadily after the third egg, and it will take at least eleven more days before the first eggs hatch. Normally, all the birds are out of the eggs within two days, and there are hardly ever any noticeable differences in size. (In exceptionally large clutches the hatching may extend to three or four days.)

## Raising the Young

Once the babies have hatched you will notice one of the parent birds sitting in front of the nest at regular intervals gagging up food and then jumping into the nest with the partner to feed the young. You can recognize the gagging clearly by the movements of the throat. And you will become aware of the tiny little nestlings within a few days. When it is quiet in the room you will be able to detect a very soft whimpering or whispering that will gradually increase in volume and soon be so loud you cannot possibly ignore it. This begging noise will from now on serve as a constant reminder of your duties.

As a substitute for maturing seeds, you will have to serve your birds fresh sprouts daily (p. 24). Mix some of the rearing food, which the birds should always have

# *Reproduction and Breeding*

This is how Zebra Finches feed the fledglings that have left the nest. The young assume the typical begging posture shown in the bird on the extreme right.

at their disposal, with a little bit of cottage cheese, egg, or grated carrot (p. 26). Don't be disappointed if the parent birds fail to respond to this treat with enthusiasm right away. Remember that Zebra Finches approach everything new with a natural suspicion. At some point, however, curiosity will win out over distrust, and the adult birds will come to expect this morning treat. If this happens before the hatching, the baby birds will benefit from it from the very first.

There is no need for you to serve the mixed soft food as soon as the lights go on in the aviary. If the parent birds start the day with some vegetarian food, this will ensure that the nestlings will not get too much animal protein, which egg and cottage cheese are rich in.

After about ten days you will notice a change in behavior. Whereas the parent birds have been completely absorbed in keeping their offspring warm and in feeding them, they now start taking some time for themselves again and occasionally even leave the babies alone for a while. The nestlings are much less dependent on their

parents for warmth at this point, because on the twelfth day their juvenile plumage, which protects them from the cold, comes in. This is the time when breeders put aluminum rings (bands) on the finches' legs. Once the young birds leave the nest, the joints of their feet are no longer thin and flexible enough to let the rings be slipped on easily. If the joints have become too large, open aluminum or plastic rings have to be used.

If they are fed properly, young Zebra Finches are ready to leave the nest after about 18 days. It never ceases to amaze me how quickly these tiny, naked, flesh-colored little creatures grow into young birds with a full set of feathers and become almost as big as their parents.

The young birds' first flying ventures are always worth watching. Zebra Finches are born knowing how to fly, but they do not instinctively know how to maneuver and land, skills they have to acquire by trial and error. A young bird will thus shoot out of the nest, make straight for the next wall, bump into it, and slide down it, fluttering wildly, to the ground. The parents will take after the fledgling immediately, calling excitedly, and then try to help it get back to the nest. The fledgling will first aim for the highest perch, flying straight up, but it usually loses its balance and plumps back to the ground. After several unsuccessful attempts it will finally manage to reach a perch and sit there for a while. Eventually the young bird will follow its parents back to the nest.

A pair of Gray Zebra Finches. The cock (right) still ▷ has the red iris of the wild strain.

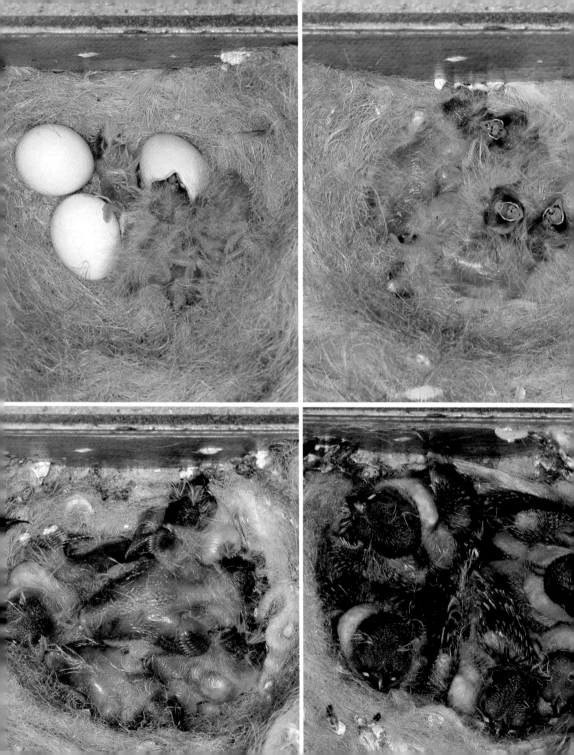

# Reproduction and Breeding

Not all the young birds leave the nest at the same time; often the process is drawn out over two or three days. Sometimes the birds that ventured out on the first day will stay in the nest the next day and will try again only on the third day along with all the rest of their fellow nestlings. Once they are all out, they soon find each other and perch close together in a long row.

Accidents such as unplanned landings in a water dish, which during this period should be filled only to a very shallow level, are quite common during these first flying ventures. Do not attempt to move the baby birds back into the nest—they are most likely to respond by jumping out again out of sheer terror. This is always a critical time, when our female Zebra Finch Fiepchen exhibits the greatest worry about her offspring. If I as much as enter the room, I am greeted by a rapid succession of short, loud warning calls. By contrast the young birds remain calm even when I observe them from quite close by; they clearly are aware that something is not as it should be, but they do not yet understand where the danger lurks. It always takes several days before they learn what the "enemy" looks like and flee from us humans.

After the fledglings leave the nest, their begging cries get even louder; the hungry young constantly harry their parents for food. It can happen that they even turn to Zebra Finches in the aviary other than their parents. An offspring of Felix and Fiepchen once hungrily approached Matz, who at that point shared their aviary, and Matz, who found it impossible to ignore the optic and acoustic stimuli of the begging baby bird, proceeded to feed it patiently.

There are four times of day when Zebra Finches feed their babies with special diligence: in the early and late morning and in the early and late afternoon. In between, the young birds sleep a lot, especially in the nest. Make it a point at one of the feedings to look carefully at the wide-open black beaks of the babies to see the color patterns that are discernible even at a distance in the oral cavity, a trait typical of the *Estrildidae*-species.

During the first few days after leaving the nest, the young Zebra Finches still need the nest for sleeping. But a week after their learning how to fly, you have to empty and clean the nesting box. Since Zebra Finches foul their nests, the back side of the nesting hollow will have a thick, half-moon-shaped layer of droppings that may plaster the nesting material to the back wall of the nesting box. This occurs because the nestlings, after their eyes open on the eighth day, turn toward the light (the entry hole) and move back a little against the back wall to drop their stool.

## The Growing Up of the Fledglings

Very soon the young Zebra Finches will start pecking on chickweed, twigs, and millet sprays even though they still beg food intermittently from their parents.

◁ The first days in the life of Zebra Finches.
Upper left and right: Nestlings on the second and fourth days after hatching.
Lower left and right: Nestlings on the eighth and twelfth days.

# Reproduction and Breeding

Eventually each young bird will succeed in husking its first seed, and from then on it will eat more and more independently. Three weeks after leaving the nest—that is, at about five to six weeks—the young birds can manage on their own, even though the parents will often go on feeding them longer.

At this point you can separate the young birds from their parents and move them to a cage of their own, but it is better to wait until the parents, about to embark on a new breeding cycle, disown their young. By this time the family ties have dissolved, and the older birds chase the younger ones to the point of exhaustion. This behavior, which may seem savage to us, also happens the other way round. If a young Zebra Finch left in a large aviary with its parents finds a partner, the young bird will attack its parents vehemently if they come too close to its chosen nesting site and compete for the site as rivals.

In no case should you sell young Zebra Finches right after they have reached independence. Give them a chance first to learn the behavior of their species, and also wait to see their splendid adult plumage emerge. The first sign of this occurs when the bill starts to change color from the root toward the tip: the black turns horn color, then orange, and later, in the fully mature male, vivid red. The black stays longest on the tip of the upper mandible. Soon after the bill, the plumage starts to change. Orange cheek spots, white and chestnut-brown markings on the side, a black band on the chest, and zebra stripes on the throat begin to show up very faintly in the young male. The young hens do not go through this temporary muddle of colors; only their bills and legs change noticeably (p. 74).

The song of the young cocks is just as imperfect as their markings. During the first few weeks of their lives, the young birds have been listening to the song of their fathers, and they are trying to imitate it. The result is a string of short, chaotic stanzas that sound like a total flop. But continued practice finally leads to success—even if there is no longer a father or any other male Zebra Finch to listen to. The young fledgling thus absorbs the song early on and later learns to reproduce it from memory. Scientists speak in this context of "imprinting" and a "sensitive period"; indeed, such learning has little in common with our usual kind of learning through trial and error.

There are many other things a young Zebra Finch absorbs during its sensitive period, such as what males and females are like and just what constitutes a member of its own species. If you sell a young Zebra Finch too early and it is then surrounded exclusively by Society Finches, it will learn to think of itself, too, as a Society Finch and refuse to have anything to do with Zebra Finches. So please wait until the young birds are a good two months old and have almost their full adult coloration. At that point, the sensitive period will be over, too, and one month later the Zebra Finches will reach sexual maturity.

One more tip: If you are not going to band the young birds, be sure the parents have bands before the young get their adult plumage, so that you will not by mistake sell one of the parents later. Or do you feel confident enough to be able to tell two

# Reproduction and Breeding

similarly colored birds from each other without chance of mistake?

## Breeding Problems

Even in the case of Zebra Finches it occasionally happens that the birds fail to breed. If you see no sign of courtship display, mating, or egg laying, check the housing conditions (temperature, light, size of cage). My first pair of Zebra Finches refused to engage in the breeding cycle until I moved them out of a cage that was too small. If all the environmental conditions are perfect and the pair are old enough, there are two possible causes for failure. One of the birds may be sterile (perhaps too old?), or, more likely, the two partners do not take to each other. In the latter case you would have to exchange one of them.

Particularly with young birds, everything may go well at first, but then they suddenly build a nest layer over the eggs or the hatchlings or start building a second nest somewhere else, letting their offspring die. Sometimes they even peck at the eggs or simply throw the nestlings out before going on to build their second nest.

The cause of such abnormal behavior may be lack of agreement between the partners or inexperience—or a scarcity of nesting material. Zebra Finches have to be able to act out fully their need for nest building. If the nest is too small or if there is not enough building material, they may develop a desire to use the material at hand over again or to work materials supplied later into the building project. So be sure to give them sufficient quantities at the beginning, and make small amounts available later in a little rack so that the birds can make minor repairs. A shortage of nesting material can also lead to plucking of the partner or even the nestlings—you will later find the plucked feathers incorporated into the nest. I have witnessed this unnatural behavior only once thus far. During his first successful reproductive cycle a cock plucked both his mate and his offspring bare around the neck to pad the nest.

If Zebra Finches breed too often and too quickly in succession, the hen in particular is weakened. The eggs also get smaller, and the quality of the young birds is affected. So try not to let your birds raise more than four broods a year. The egg production is less strenuous for the hen than is the raising of the baby birds; you can therefore simply replace the clutch with white ceramic or plastic eggs of similar size. If you do this too early, the hen will usually go on laying until there is a full clutch. Sometimes the absence of nesting material can also prevent a new brood. But Zebra Finches always have to have a sleeping nest in which to spend the night.

## What You Should Know about the Different Color Strains

All Zebra Finches bred (for show) in Europe are descendants of the Australian race of Zebra Finches. Timor Zebra Finches, which occur only on the Lesser Sunda Islands, were probably crossed in only rarely

49

# Reproduction and Breeding

and more by accident than intent. Through the still ongoing process of domestication, our Zebra Finches have changed from the original wild form to the extent that our common gray strain is already clearly distinguishable from its wild cousin.

But the strains developed during the last few decades differ from the wild type not only in color but also in shape. The standard set down by the Toledo Bird Association Zebra Finch Club of America, Inc. (c/o Ms. Ann Scharbach, Sec., 5432 303 Street, Toledo, OH 43611) lists the size, type, posture, wing, tail, leg and bill shape, as well as the color and markings of an ideal Zebra Finch, calling for qualities that are well beyond those of wild Zebra Finches. The Zebra Finches you see at shows are up to almost one inch (2 centimeters) larger than wild birds. The desirable teardrop type (p. 8) that is called for in all color strains is in fact modeled on the shape of wild Zebra Finches, but it is often difficult to achieve, because breeding for color as well as for commercial production often results in less-robust birds with a poor shape or type. Many new color variations show hereditary defects at least initially, such as sensitivity to cold or light, generally greater susceptibility to deficiency diseases, and even blindness and malformations.

Some few strains cannot even multiply successfully among themselves. Purebred offspring tend to degenerate and diminish in size or, as dominant mutations, die at the embryonic or nestling stage. In the case of other variations (combination colors), each bird is the result of crossing two strains, which have to be bred separately.

## Advice to the Beginner

Most color variations are achieved by diluting the ground color and markings (p. 52); in other words, the variations are not, properly speaking, new colors but simply less color. (An animal that is lacking all color pigmentation is called an *albino*.)

All cultivated color strains are based on mutations—that is, changes in the genetic makeup—that also occur in nature. But in nature these changes do not last long, because the (dominant) natural coloring reasserts itself against the new, "unnatural" colors. The prime reason for this occurrence has to do with the survival of the species. Light-colored (white) birds are easier for predators to spot; also, a wild-colored female will always opt for a male with fully developed, bright-display plumage (p. 72). Suitors of different, more muted plumage will be considered "colorless fellows" and not have a chance.

I should like to offer a few pointers to anyone embarking on his or her first ventures in breeding Zebra Finches for certain colors or for show:

• Restrict yourself to one or two strains so that you can concentrate your efforts.

• Begin with a color that has already been bred extensively and is relatively free from problems, such as gray (or normal), fawn, pied or variegated, or white.

• Try to stay away from the risks described previously in breeding for certain colors. Do not engage in dangerous experiments simply out of curiosity or ignorance.

• Keep a record book in which you enter everything about each individual brood, such as length of incubation, time spent in the nest, development of adult coloration, genetic makeup, and color.

Learn everything you can about the individual strains; this includes an adequate knowledge of genetics. In the two sections that follow I can give you only a superficial introduction to these complex topics in the hope of motivating you to study them more intensively.

## How Are the Colors Passed On?

Genetics is a large and complex field of study, but most people have at least heard of the laws of genetics and of their discoverer, Johann Gregor Mendel. Perhaps you also know that the carriers of genetic information inside the cell nucleus are called chromosomes and that human beings have a double set of these in all their normal body cells. In addition to the regular chromosome pairs, the body cells have two sex chromosomes, which are designated XX in a woman and XY in a man. Chromosomes are bent, rodlike structures that are made up of many different units, called genes. Since both chromosomes of each chromosome pair (including the XX pair) are identical, the genes in the matching locations contain genetic information for the same trait. All genes therefore exist in duplicate except for the genes in the reproductive cells, which have only one set of chromosomes. When an egg cell is fertilized, two single chromosome sets recombine into a new, normal double set, the beginning of a new living being.

This process functions exactly the same way in Zebra Finches as it does in human beings, with only one small difference: In birds it is the hen that has the XY chromosomes. Depending on which chromosome half unites with a male reproductive cell, the resulting chick will be either a cock (XX) or a hen (XY). Take a look at the following diagram:

| ♂ \ ♀ | X | Y | = hen |
|---|---|---|---|
| = male  X | XX | XY | } = chicks |
| X | XX | XY | |

As you can see, there are four possible combinations, always producing half males and half females. The same diagram works for predicting the results of a simple crossing of colors. Let us assume you want to mate a normal Gray Zebra Finch with a white one. Genetically, gray (the wild coloration) is usually dominant over other colors, and white is therefore recessive. What you are doing is crossing a dominant trait (GG for gray) with a recessive one (ww for white) with each reproductive cell carrying either a G or a w gene. The result of this crossing is four Gw's:

| | w | w |
|---|---|---|
| G | Gw | Gw |
| G | Gw | Gw |

When the young birds develop their adult coloration, only gray, the dominant trait, manifests itself externally; it is therefore represented by a capital letter. The offspring, then, are all gray, but they are not homozygous (i.e., both genes carrying the same genetic information) but rather

# *Reproduction and Breeding*

heterozygous (i.e., one gene for gray, the other for white). This can be represented by using a capital and a lower case letter (Gw) or by using a slash: gray/white: gray, split for white. Geneticists also use the terms *genotype* for the genetic makeup of an organism and *phenotype* for the external appearance of the organism. The results are more varied and interesting when you start crossing first-generation offspring of gray and white parents:

|   | G  | w  |
|---|----|----|
| G | GG | Gw |
| w | Gw | ww |

If you have bought two Gray Zebra Finches and suddenly find a white chick among their offspring, you will now understand why.

There is no external (phenotypical) difference between birds with heterozygous (Gw) and homozygous (GG) genes. A recessive trait shows up only if there are two genes (ww) for it. And in the case of some mutations, two dominant genes lead to the death of the organism.

Finally, you should know about hereditary factors that are sex linked, some of which also play a role in human genetics (e.g., color blindness and hemophilia). The X chromosome of a Zebra Finch hen may contain a gene for the color fawn, for instance, but the Y chromosome, which is smaller, lacks the corresponding gene for fawn or gray. That is why a fawn hen can carry genetic information only for the color fawn $(f-)$, whereas a male can either be purebred fawn (ff) or be gray in appearance but have heterozygous genes (Gf).

My fawn male and his gray mate therefore will always produce fawn hens and gray, heterozygous cocks:

|   | G  | (Y)  |
|---|----|------|
| f | Gf | $f-$ |
| f | Gf | $f-$ |

In records of animal breeding, males are usually designated with numbers such as 1,0 (or 2,0, 3,0) and females with 0,1, etc. Thus a breeder of Zebra Finches would read the statement "2,2 gray" to mean "two gray pairs."

## The Most Important Color Strains

Since almost all traits derived from mutations can be combined, there are at this point, in theory, 58 different color variations. Most of these are combinations of gray and fawn. To make clear the deviations from the wild form, I will start this description of the most common strains with a description of wild Zebra Finches.

*Natural coloration.* Zebra Finches living in the wild measure about 4¼ inches (11 centimeters) and have eyes with a bright red iris. The markings on the face show a clear black and white contrast, the gray back has a slight brown tinge, and the belly is white even in the female. This wild form of the Zebra Finch is no longer found in cages and aviaries, because Australia has legally prohibited the export of wild animals. Timor Zebra Finches are still imported occasionally. These birds are smaller than the Australian race, have a narrower chest band and hardly any zebra markings above

# Reproduction and Breeding

the band. The top of the head is brownish. When mated with gray, this coloration is recessive, and these birds should therefore be purebred. It is hard to comprehend that judges at bird shows often rate this still completely natural strain lower than artificial breeds of Zebra Finches.

*Gray, or Normal.* Gray Zebra Finches are closest to wild Zebra Finches in appearance. But the iris is dark and hardly visible, the belly of the female is beige, and her facial markings are often somewhat darker. The back is a purer gray than that of the wild bird or, in the case of poor specimens, brownish. The standard calls for a slate-gray back, the reason this strain is called gray. Unfortunately, many Gray Zebra Finches these days are no longer homozygous but carry hidden recessive characteristics.

*Fawn.* This color originated through a change in the chemical structure of the pigment (p. 66). It also occurs occasionally in the wild. Fawn forms a new ground color that together with gray gives rise to many different color variants. As mentioned before, fawn coloring is a sex-linked trait.

*Pied or Variegated.* Pied markings occur when pigment is present in only some parts of the plumage. Since no pied Zebra Finch looks exactly like any other, you can expect to find new patterns in every brood. The pied factor is passed on recessively but dominates over white.

*White.* This color is caused by a total absence of color pigment except in the dark eyes. These birds are therefore not albinos, because true albinos have red eyes. Because of differences in behavior, you

should not keep White Zebra Finches together with other pairs of Zebra Finches (p. 73).

*White ticked.* Here the white has a faint gray (or fawn) overlay caused by the colored tips of the feathers. It is not yet clear how this trait is genetically transmitted.

*Masked white or chestnut-flanked white.* A white-to-cream-colored bird with the markings still faintly visible. This coloration is a sex-linked trait, and achieving it in purebred form is questionable.

*Pale back.* This mutation, like fawn color, is based on a sex-linked factor.

*Silver or dilute normal.* The silvery impression is created by a dilution of the melanin pigment of Gray Zebra Finches. Silver birds should never be mated with each other, because silver is a dominant factor and results in death if present in purebred (homozygous) form.

*Cream.* This is a fainter shade of fawn brought about by the combination of fawn and silver. Mating cream with cream or cream with silver therefore does not produce the desired result, but mating cream and fawn does.

*Black breast.* In these birds the black chest band is enlarged, extending up to the throat, but the tear stripe and the tail bands have vanished. This mutation is especially sensitive to the cold.

*Penguin.* The belly and the face are without markings, that is, they are white. The back is gray or fawn. Periodic crossbreedings with these two colors are necessary to prevent degeneration.

*Light breast.* This strain looks like the penguin strain, but the color of the back and the zebra markings and tail bands are fainter. Like the cream strain, the light breast should be crossbred with fawn.

*Yellow beak.* This trait is recessive; consequently, the bills are either red or yellow, without intermediate shades.

*Crested.* This is not a color variant but a hereditary mutation affecting the scalp, producing a flat swirl of feathers. The trait is dominant, and birds with monozygous genes for it (crest x crest) are not viable.

*Lead-cheeked and Orange-breasted Zebra Finches.* Birds of these strains are often blind or have other genetic defects.

Many other combinations exist, such as *black breast* (gray or fawn) with pied markings or crest or a yellow bill.

# If Your Zebra Finches Get Sick

## Prevention Is the Best Cure

If you create a proper, clean, and safe environment for your Zebra Finches and feed them correctly, you are not likely to run into health problems with your birds. Most illnesses—especially those affecting the organs of the respiratory and digestive systems, as well as fractures, wounds, and infections—are frequently caused by mistakes or carelessness on the part of the keeper.

Preventive care is therefore not only the moral (and legal) duty of anyone keeping birds, but it is also simpler and cheaper than medical treatment. Also, it may in many cases be the only chance of survival for these tiny birds. All small birds and mammals use a great deal of energy compared to their size and therefore have to feed constantly. If an illness weakens a Zebra Finch or keeps it from eating, it will in most cases die quickly. To help your Zebra Finches overcome a possible illness, daily observation is therefore crucial. If you detect any sign of illness you must immediately determine the cause, try to remedy it, and initiate treatment as soon as possible.

## General Signs of Illness

You can easily tell a Zebra Finch that is not feeling well by its listless behavior. The bird is inactive, sits on its perch apathetically and usually alone, often turning its head to the back, eyes closed. If a bird is sick, it will puff up its feathers for warmth and sit horizontally, its belly close

to the perch. In a very serious case the finch will sit on the ground. The eyes are either half-open or closed, and often the body rises and falls slightly with each labored breath.

These symptoms, which acompany many illnesses, should cause you immediate alarm. If you recognize a disease in time, your bird may have a chance to survive. Of course, not every Zebra Finch hunkered down on its belly to take a nap is sick; careful observation will quickly teach you the difference.

## First Measures

There are three first steps you can take immediately without specialized knowledge:

• Isolate the bird in a hospital cage (p. 56) so that other birds will not chase it and will also not get infected. Housing the ill

A bird that sits on the ground with feathers fluffed up and eyes squeezed shut is sick and needs to be treated right away.

bird separately also makes it easier to administer treatment.

• Shine an infrared or heat lamp on the bird. This makes up for loss of warmth, increases circulation, and stimulates the production of antibodies. A heat lamp is not recommended, however, after accidents that cause fractures.

• Put the bird on a convalescent diet and increase the vitamin intake. Many illnesses are caused by vitamin deficiencies that can be corrected with multivitamins. Some brands also contain amino acids, minerals, and trace elements. Some diseases (infections, parasite infestations) lead to diarrhea. A diet of dry birdseed (spray millet) and water or diluted camomile tea helps clear up intestinal problems, and charcoal removes poisons from the intestine. Resume giving soft food and fresh food, as well as sand, only after several days. At that point you should also discontinue the charcoal to let the medication or vitamins be fully effective.

## The Hospital Cage

Isolate your sick bird in a reserve cage that you enclose on three sides with cloth and in front of which you mount an infrared lamp. Since high air humidity together with warmth speeds recovery, it is best to moisten the cloth. Box cages (p. 10) make excellent hospital cages; they have mesh at the top, and you can thus shine the infrared light on the birds from above.

Pet stores also sell very convenient hospital boxes that are equipped with heat lamps,

thermostats, and hygrometers and can be closed off at the front with a sliding plexiglass panel (useful for inhalation treatments). These boxes come in two sizes: 18 × 16 × 26 inches (45 × 40 × 66 cm) and 34 × 17 × 20½ inches (85 × 42.5 × 52 cm). The same manufacturers also sell cheaper models without all the accessories and made of synthetic material (16¼ or 20½ inches [41 or 51 centimeters] long), but

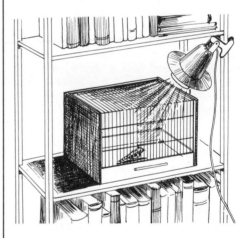

For many illnesses, exposing the bird to a heat lamp aids the healing process.

because of the low solid tops, heat and infrared light can be administered only from the front.

To keep the birds from getting too hot, only half the cage should be exposed to the heat source, and even there the temperature should never rise above 86° to 95°F (30° to 35°C). The bird can then move to the cooler

# If Your Zebra Finches Get Sick

half as needed. The heat lamp should be on day and night. If you use an infrared light, you can leave off the night light that Zebra Finches ordinarily need at night, but make sure the sick bird can see enough to find food even at night. The patient will need absolute quiet and should therefore be located far enough from its fellows so that it cannot hear them.

## A Medicine Cabinet for Birds

An aviculturist should always have some basic supplies and medications on hand in case the birds become ill. Included should be an infrared or heat lamp of 100 to 150 watts, a bottle of multivitamins (if you do not habitually use them for your birds), charcoal for birds, coagulant cotton, iodine or another wound disinfectant, a pipette for giving liquid medicines, small scissors, bandages or heavy thread, toenail clippers, an insecticide for ectoparasites, insecticide strips as a preventive measure, and a disinfectant for the aviary and accessories. Two other important items are a book on bird diseases and the address of a veterinarian who specializes in small birds.

Broad-spectrum antibiotics (Terramycin, Aureomycin) and sulfonamides are prescription drugs and keep only for a limited time. They must be used only against a specific illness (never as a preventive measure) and have to be given in doses that reflect the specific body weight. (A Zebra Finch weighs only about 13 grams.) Generally, the five-day treatment should not be cut short, and vitamin supplements have to be given simultaneously (p. 29).

## The Trip to the Veterinarian

In small birds, serious illness quickly results in death (p. 55). That is why, as I have already said, quick help is so important. You do not have much time to figure out the correct diagnosis, let alone try various cures. If it is not obvious what the problem is or how it should be treated, only a veterinarian can help.

A veterinarian that specializes in small household pets or birds is likely to have some experience with exotic finches. He or she is the best doctor for your sick Zebra Finch. To keep from frightening your bird any more than necessary, transport it to the doctor's office well protected against cold and drafts in a hospital box. There the veterinarian can observe the little patient and examine its droppings.

## Diseases and Their Treatment

Very few bird diseases are accompanied by unmistakable and typical symptoms, and the catalog of symptoms on page 58 lists a number of possible causes under each entry. This list will be of use to you not only in trying to determine specific illnesses but also in talking with the veterinarian, who, after all, often depends on your observations in making the diagnosis.

### Colds
*Causes:* Exposure to drafts; cold; cool, damp air; sudden drops in temperature that can lower the resistance to cold germs so much that the bird gets sick.

# List of the Most Important Symptoms of Illness

| Symptoms | Diagnosis |
|---|---|
| Drooping wing; unsuccessful attempts at flying | Broken wing |
| Dragging leg | Broken leg |
| Unable to balance on perch; resting on belly; hopping falteringly | Broken leg or partial paralysis |
| Getting tangled (on wire mesh or in nesting material) | Overgrown nails; incorrect or overly long nesting materials |
| Discolorations and swellings on toes | Gangrene; inflamed joints; infection |
| Twisting of toes and legs | Rickets; lack of vitamins and exercise; injuries; inflamed joints |
| Deformation of bill | Overgrowth of horny part of bill |
| Lethargy; lameness; twisting of head; cramps; twitching; staggering | Concussion; vitamin deficiency (usually B, more rarely E); infection; poisoning |
| Thickening of legs and toes with prominent scales | Excessive growth of keratinous tissue; burrowing mites (mange) |
| Bald spots (especially on head and neck) | Open wounds that were not stitched; hormone imbalances; deficiency diseases; feather pulling by other birds; external parasites; molt caused by fight |
| Continued dropping of a few feathers without causing bare patches | Molt. Not a disease, but serves the necessary renewal of plumage. |
| Nervousness; pecking at feathers; violent scratching; continued restlessness even at night | Red bird mites (very common), which are actually on the bird only at night; feather mites; lice |
| Lethargy, shortness of breath; exhaustion | Obesity (and liver damage) |
| Discharge of pus from nose; plugged nostrils | Cold; infections; poisonous vapors |
| Labored breathing with bill wide open; noisy breathing; general symptoms of serious disease | Cold; infections; airsac mites and other parasites (Filaria) |
| Diarrhea; runny, brownish, greenish, or yellowish droppings, sometimes bloody; lack of appetite; moist, inflamed cloaca | Intestinal disorder; cold; infections involving bacteria or fungi; viruses; parasites (coccidia, worms) |
| Difficulty passing stool; enlarged, hard, and partially bloody droppings; general symptoms of illness | Constipation (rare); blockage of intestine caused by egg binding or hernia of oviduct |
| Fruitless pressing followed by shortness of breath, apathy, exhaustion, and lameness of legs | Egg binding |
| Oviduct hanging out of cloaca | Prolapsed oviduct |

# If Your Zebra Finches Get Sick

*Treatment:* Move the bird to the hospital box and supply heat, vitamins, and a convalescent diet to combat the cold and intestinal problems that often accompany colds. If the vet has prescribed antibiotics, carefully give the bird the exact dose of the liquid medicine with a pipette.

## Intestinal Disorders
*Causes:* Colds, spoiled or contaminated food, dirty or germ-infested water (see "Infections" and "Endoparasites").
*Treatment:* Isolate the bird in a hospital cage, supply heat and vitamins (especially B vitamins), feed a convalescent diet, give camomile tea (diluted and lukewarm) and antibiotics (see "Colds"). Some bacteria (salmonella) and parasites (coccidiae) that cause intestinal problems are highly dangerous, and their presence cannot be diagnosed by the layperson; therefore, a veterinarian should be consulted.

## Infections
Birds are subject to bacterial (salmonella), fungal, and viral infections.
*Causes:* The prime cause is food or water contaminated with salmonella. But these pathogens can also be introduced by wild birds, mice, rats, and flies, as well as by newly purchased birds. They can also be transmitted to other animals and to human beings. If there is any suspicion of salmonella, a stool sample should be examined by the veterinarian or at an animal clinic.
*Treatment:* The infected bird must be isolated immediately to keep the disease from spreading to the other birds. Depending on the diagnosis, the veterinarian will prescribe antibiotics or other medication (for viruses). Additional vitamins are beneficial in any case.

## Endoparasites
This is the term used to describe parasites living inside the host's body, and it thus includes coccidiae and other protozoans (one-celled organisms) as well as worms (e.g., Filaria).
*Causes:* These parasites can be introduced by new birds just like bacteria (see "Infections"), or they can be picked up from contaminated soil.
*Treatment:* Endoparasites can place your entire flock in danger. Once their specific nature has been diagnosed (through microscopic examination of a stool sample), sulfonamides are given in the drinking water. The five-day treatment should be repeated after a three-day pause, to make sure the pests are completely eliminated. Dirty soil has to be replaced, in an outdoor aviary to the full depth of a spade. Insecticide strips used according to instructions also help against airsac mites.

## Ectoparasites
These are external parasites, such as mites and lice, that make the birds nervous and cause them to pull feathers.
*Causes:* Introduction through newly purchased or native birds that are infested. Cracks, grooves, and dark corners are breeding grounds of mites. The common red bird mite is usually found on birds only at night, but it can also affect humans. If

you cover the cage with a white cloth overnight, you will see lots of tiny dark dots, the mites, on it in the morning. Only weakened birds suffer from the common feather mites.

*Treatment:* Place neck ruffs made of paper on birds affected with ectoparasites and dust or paint the birds with a safe insecticide even if only the legs require treatment (against burrowing mites). The entire aviary (including perches and nests) has to be thoroughly disinfected, and the birds must be moved out while this is being done. Hanging insecticide strips in the room helps prevent reinfestation.

## Constipation

*Causes:* The bird may have swallowed too much sand and grit or eaten hard dry seeds too exclusively so that the intestinal walls have become distended.

*Treatment:* Withhold sand, grit, and dry seeds for one day, provide sprouts, and feed a few drops of mineral oil or olive oil.

## Egg Binding

*Causes:* The female may be too young; the environmental conditions may be poor (too confined, cold, or wet); the eggshells may be too soft because of vitamin and calcium deficiency.

*Treatment:* Build up the robustness of the female through use of a heat lamp (p. 56), and let an experienced veterinarian remove the egg. The gravest danger is that the difficulty in laying the egg will cause the oviduct to protrude from the cloaca. If this

happens, only the vet can save the bird, who should then be kept from trying to breed again.

## Liver Damage, Obesity

*Causes:* Spoiled food (as in the case of intestinal disorders) or food high in calories but low in vitamins together with insufficient exercise. Too much fat and too much protein from animal sources also negatively affect the development of young seed-eaters.

*Treatment:* Provide a balanced diet (p. 22); give the bird plenty of chance to exercise.

## Gangrene

*Causes:* Injuries; frostbite; burns; lack of circulation (caused by bands that are too tight).

*Treatment:* This condition can be halted but not cured by applying a salve in the case of frostbite or, ultimately, by amputating the decayed tissue.

## Inflamed Joints

*Causes:* Lack of movement; infection; improper perches.

*Treatment:* Provide flexible natural branches of varying thickness; give the bird plenty of chance to exercise.

## Rickets

*Causes:* Insufficient amounts of vitamin D, calcium, and phosphorus in the early days (pp. 26–29).

# If Your Zebra Finches Get Sick

*Treatment:* This condition can be halted but not cured by supplying vitamins and minerals (primarily calcium).

## Motor Disturbances

These disturbances can take the form of twitching, staggering, turning in circles, cramps, and paralysis; they indicate a disorder of the nervous system.
*Causes:* Infections (viral); poisons; nutritional deficiencies (lack of vitamin B or E).
*Treatment:* Disorders caused by viruses are, at this point, rarely curable.
Deficiency diseases can often be successfully treated through a diet high in vitamins, protein, and minerals. Give additional vitamin supplements and try to keep the bird from getting excited or frightened.

## Bleeding

*Causes:* Accidental injuries; fights. Internal bleeding can be caused by bumping against something with the head, by poisoning, or by a lack of vitamin K.
*Treatment:* Stop the bleeding with coagulant cotton and disinfect the wound with iodine.
Exotic finches cannot afford much loss of blood. If you suspect internal bleeding, make sure the bird is kept absolutely quiet in the hospital cage.

## Fractures

*Causes:* Panicked flying in the dark or in an inappropriate cage; flying against a window; being struck by the frame of the bird net; catching a foot in nesting material that is too long.
*Treatment:* Even wild Zebra Finches are disabled amazingly little by broken legs. Fractures of the upper and lower thigh and injuries to the knees and toes are usually left alone even if the bones grow together crookedly. A broken leg should be splinted with a piece of straw slit lengthwise, some woolen thread, and plaster (or glue). Either you or the veterinarian can do this, and the splint should stay on two to three weeks.
If part of the leg hangs by only a piece of skin or tendon it is better to amputate it. Stop the bleeding with coagulant cotton and disinfect the stump with iodine.

You cannot put a splint on the broken wing of an exotic finch. All you can do is to tape both wings to the body in their natural position and tie the tips of the wings together at the tail (for three to four weeks). The results of this treatment vary.

This is the right way to hold a bird for clipping its claws.

# If Your Zebra Finches Get Sick

## Overgrown Toenails
*Causes:* Perches that are too thin; insufficient wear of the nails.
*Treatment:* Trim the nails, preferably with nail clippers. Hold the toes up against the light and be careful not to injure the blood vessels that show up dark in the light-colored nail.

## Overgrowth of the Bill
*Causes:* Vitamin and mineral deficiency; not enough wearing down.
*Treatment:* File the excessive growth carefully with a nail file.

## Bald Spots
*Causes:* Hormone imbalances, deficiency diseases (lack of vitamin A), feather pulling caused by lack of activity and exercise (boredom, stress in a cage that is too small); lack of sunlight, and air humidity that is too low (p. 15); fights over nesting territory; incompatibility of a pair; perhaps also a deficiency of certain substances that the bird seeks to obtain in the feathers. At brooding time, a shortage of nesting materials can also cause feather pulling. And sometimes there can be a kind of molt out of fright. If you grab a bird by the tail, for instance, it might fly off, leaving the feathers in your hand.
*Treatment:* Correct the situation that causes the problem.

Zebra Finches in their natural habitat. ▷
Above left: A male Zebra Finch inspecting a nesting cavity; Above right: Two pairs of a flock.
Below: A Zebra Finch drinking water by sucking it up.

# *Understanding Zebra Finches*

## Zebra Finches and Their Family

Zebra Finches belong to the family of Waxbills, Mannikins, Munias, and allied species (*Estrildidae*), which, together with many other families (e.g., Weaver Finches, Whydahs, true finches), are part of the large order Passeriformes, commonly known as Passerines or perching birds, and of the suborder Passeres. The striking feature of *Estrildidae*-species is not their song but their colorful plumage, which has made some of these small birds so popular with aviculturists. There are about 125 species of *Estrildidae*; scientists are not yet in agreement on all details of classification. *Estrildidae*-species can be subdivided into two major tribes, namely, the thinner-billed species (*Estrildini*, or Waxbills) that live in Africa, and the stouter-billed ones (*Amadini*, or Munias and Mannikins) native to Australia, southern Asia, and—in some cases—to Africa as well.

The Australian Zebra Finch, belonging to the second group, is therefore a Mannikin, or better still, a *grass* finch. Its scientific name is *Taeniopygia guttata castanotis*. The first word indicates the genus, the second identifies the species within the genus (in this case the genus has only one species), and the last gives the subspecies or race. A second race of the species inhabits the Lesser Sunda Islands north of

Australia and is called the Timor Zebra Finch. Because this subspecies was discovered first, the trinomial name includes a repetition of the species name: *Taeniopygia guttata guttata*. Some scientists assign the Zebra Finch to the genus *Poephila*. English, Dutch, Danish, Swedish, and German breeders often refer to Zebra Finches simply as "zebras."

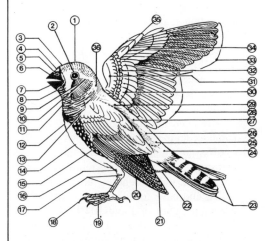

What is where on a Zebra Finch? Knowing the different parts of the body and the areas of plumage is especially useful when talking with your veterinarian. 1 Crown, 2 Eye, 3 Forehead, 4 Base of bill, 5 Nostrils, 6 Upper mandible, 7 Lower mandible, 8 Chin, 9 Cheek or side of the head, 10 Ear coverts 11 Throat, 12 Breast, 13 Shoulder, 14 Abdomen, 15 Flank or side, 16 Lower thigh, 17 Tarsal joint (above) and tarsus or leg (below), 18 Claws or toenails, 19 Toes, 20 Cloaca, 21 Primaries, 22 Under tail coverts, 23 Tail feathers, 24 Upper tail coverts, 25 Rump, 26 Lower back, 27 Back, 28 Secondaries, 29 Upper back, 30 Secondary coverts, 31 Marginal wing coverts, 32 Lesser wing coverts, 33 Primaries, 34 Primary coverts, 35 Bastard wing, 36 Nape.

◁ Above: Australian Zebra Finches share their habitat with budgerigars, cockatiels, and doves (Diamond dove at right)
Below: Zebra Finches bathing in shallow water.

# Understanding Zebra Finches

## Anatomy of a Zebra Finch

Birds are vertebrates that evolved from reptiles a long time ago. They are distinguished from all other classes of animals by having feathers that cover almost the entire body. The forelimbs have become modified into wings.

## The Plumage

The contour feathers give a bird its distinctive shape and color: the large wing and tail feathers enable the bird to fly and maneuver, and the smaller body feathers supply the necessary streamlined shape.

The vanes of a feather consist of many barbs branching off the shaft and of interlocking barbules.

Before the contour feathers come in, a nestling grows downy feathers that protect the body from the cold. Birds can also counteract temperature fluctuations actively by puffing up their feathers and thus increasing the insulation the plumage provides. Birds, unlike reptiles, are warm-blooded and have to maintain a constant body temperature of about 104°F (40°C). Unlike our native songbirds, exotic finches can adapt to lower temperatures only to a very limited degree.

Fully grown feathers are made up of keratin and are dead. Although very tough, they do wear down from constant use. Birds therefore replace plumage at regular intervals—that is, they molt. That is why you keep finding feathers on the bottom of the aviary and on your rug, especially when the young birds have just reached maturity.

For the breeder of Zebra Finches the colors of the plumage are of greatest interest. These colors are the result of color pigments in the feathers. In chemical terms, the coloration of Zebra Finches is due to two forms of the pigment melanin: the black eumelanin (mostly in the feather barbules) and the reddish brown phaeomelanin (mostly in the branches or barbs).

A high concentration of eumelanin creates the black markings, while pure phaeomelanin results in the orange cheeks and sides of the Zebra Finch. Both types of melanin can occur in diluted form or mixed and thus give rise to new colors. Most of the many different color strains are the result of a diluting or total absence of melanin in the feathers, but melanin can also occur in higher concentration or in another chemical form, or it can be present in a different pigment pattern.

## The Bill and Limbs

Lipochromes (fatty pigments) are responsible for the red color of the bill and legs of Zebra Finches as well as for the bright red iris of the wild birds. (The eyes of domesticated Zebra Finches are at this point generally dark.) The bill is clearly a darker red in the cock than in the hen. The bill serves a bird not only as the major tool for dealing with food and holding on to things but also as a weapon. It is particularly important that the bill be well adapted to the kind of foods the bird eats. Since Zebra Finches feed primarily on grass seeds, the upper mandible of the bill is domed for holding seeds. For cutting seeds, there is a sharp ridge in the center of the mandible with some secondary ridges that end in a hump at the back of the mouth. The seeds that are being hulled rest in the lower mandible and are moved rapidly back and forth. Each individual grain is rolled against the central ridge of the upper mandible until both halves of the husk have fallen off.

Since birds do not have sweat glands, they open their bills and pant when they get hot. The moisture that evaporates in the oral cavity helps them cool down.

Do you know where the knee of a bird is located? The backward-pointing joints in your Zebra Finch's legs are not knees bending the wrong way; they are tarsal joints corresponding to the human heel. Birds thus do not walk (or hop) on their feet but on their toes. The knee connecting the upper and lower leg lies very close to the body and is hidden by the side plumage.

## Internal and Sensory Organs

Nature invented a unique solution when she created the avian lung: The subdividing bronchial tubes do not come to a dead end but instead pass the air into "air sacs,"

some of which even penetrate into the bones, thus reducing the weight of the bird. When the air returns from the air sacs in the process of exhalation, it passes through the lungs a second time and is thus used twice.

The kidneys of Zebra Finches retain almost all the water the birds drink. This is an excellent adaptive mechanism to the semi-arid habitat of these birds.

Unlike mammals, birds urinate and defecate in the same motion at the same time. The feces drop first, immediately followed by the urine. The feces are tubular in shape, soft, yet formed. The urine is a combination of a clear, transparent liquid and urates, which are pasty and white. The water content of the urine depends upon the water content of the diet, the total amount of water in the body, and, very importantly, the normal functioning of the organs—most notably, the kidneys and the liver. It is primarily the kidneys that regulate the urine volume. If the body has more water than it needs, more is excreted, causing the urine to contain more water. If the body has less water than required, it conserves what it has by excreting a drier urine.

On the lower back near the base of the tail there is an oil gland (uropygium), whose fatty secretion the birds rub into their feathers to keep them elastic and waterproof.

Most birds see and hear with great acuity; their sense of taste is quite good, but their sense of smell is less well developed. Unlike human beings, birds do not have three-dimensional vision, because only one of the eyes, which are located on the sides of

# Understanding Zebra Finches

the head, can see an object at any one time. But their field of vision is very wide. The eyelids shut by moving up from below.

## Habitat and Distribution

Of all the grass finches, the Zebra Finch is the most common and widely distributed in Australia. It inhabits the entire dry interior, except for some wet coastal forests.

Four environmental factors determine where Zebra Finches can live: temperature, rainfall, vegetation, and availability of watering places.

Zebra Finches can withstand not only very hot temperatures but, considering that they are exotic grass finches, also surprisingly low ones. Only when it gets below 43°F (6°C) is it too cold for them. (For brooding they need temperatures of at least 54°F [12°C]).

Zebra Finches raise their young primarily on ripening seeds, and that presupposes enough rain to make the grass grow. On the other hand, they cannot live in high air humidity and constant wetness, because they are basically creatures of dry habitats. Since rainfalls are unpredictable in their native regions, their mating is not tied to any particular season; they have to start their breeding cycle as soon as it is warm enough and as soon as the first (or last) showers of a rainy spell occur. Consequently, Zebra Finches are prepared to mate at all times of the year and to proceed with the business of raising a family without wasting time.

Adaptation to the climate of the Australian steppes explains not only the distribution of Zebra Finches but also the reason they have not penetrated to certain areas. Along the cool southern coast (Adelaide), either it is too cold or the rain falls in winter so that there is not much vegetation growth in the warm summertime. In the extreme northeast (Cape York Peninsula), on the other hand, it is quite warm but too humid, and there is too much rain.

In the rest of Australia, Zebra Finches are found near watering places, which the birds often visit hourly to drink and bathe, although they can manage for several weeks without water if necessary. Zebra Finches inhabit only open steppes with scattered clumps of bushes and trees, never the denser forests in the eastern part of the continent.

In the more heavily populated areas of Australia, Zebra Finches have become homophilic, that is, they have adapted to and benefited from human activity. They have been able to thrive where man created artificial watering places in arid areas (cattle troughs) and cut down large forests to turn the land into fields and pastures.

## The Behavior of Zebra Finches

Zebra Finches are extremely gregarious birds that are never met singly in their native habitat but always found in groups of several pairs. The closest bond is the one between cock and hen; these two set off together to find food and drink, and to bathe; they preen themselves together, and rest and spend the night cuddled up next to each other. They do things separately only while the eggs and the nestlings have to be kept warm. Young birds usually sit close to each other in long rows. Adult females indulge in body contact with each other only rarely, and males in full coloration, never.

## Flocks and Colonies

At times of drought Zebra Finches often combine in huge flocks to search for food and water. Under more clement conditions they spend the entire year in smaller flocks of fifty to a hundred birds and stay in one place. Such a flock may be composed of several smaller associations, most of whose members know each other individually and maintain a brood colony somewhat removed from the flock's steady location. This is the place where the birds have their sleeping nests and where the pairs also build their brood nests. The latter are rarely found next to each other; if there are enough trees and bushes, each pair claims a separate one.

Each flock is also made up of small groups of at least three pairs, which generally nest together as friendly neighbors in the same colony.

As soon as day breaks, the Zebra Finches emerge from their nests, gather together, and set off for the meeting place of the flock, which may be several thousand yards away. Then the entire flock sets out in search of food. In the course of the day some of the birds keep returning to their colonies to sit on eggs or feed the young. Two hours before sunset there is one more great gathering of the flock before the groups take off for their colonies to sleep in their nests.

## Preening

Pairs of Zebra Finches not only preen themselves simultaneously, but the partners also preen each other. Since the birds can only scratch their heads, necks, and throats but not preen them, they invite their partners to take over in these places, and the partners understand these requests immediately. One bird will thus groom the head of the other—who obviously enjoys these attentions—for minutes at a time. Only if one partner scratches too vigorously or in the wrong spot will it be stopped and reprimanded.

In the course of preening, Zebra Finches periodically scratch themselves with rapid motions. They lean a little to one side to keep their balance while standing on one leg and move the free foot up behind the

In order to scratch its head, a Zebra Finch reaches up with its foot behind the wing.

wing to scratch a few strokes with their toenails.

Repeated grooming (p. 36) is essential to keep the plumage in good shape and is thus of vital importance. Bathing serves the same purpose. When the birds plunge their breasts into the water and wiggle their bottoms, the water splashes onto the back and head. Afterwards they sit on a branch, shake themselves, and place each feather where it belongs.

## Feeding

Like some other exotic finches living in dry climates, Zebra Finches have developed a quick and efficient method of drinking. They do not lift their heads for each swallow to run down the throat the way most small birds do. Instead they suck up the water.

The most important daily activity of birds is the search for food. Zebra Finches live primarily on grasses, though they also eat the seed of dicotyledons (plants with two seed leaves). They pick up grass seeds off the ground as well as quartz particles, charcoal, and (sometimes) grains of salt. Grains are also pecked out of standing stalks of grass and foxtail millet. If the stalks are too tall for the birds to reach the seeds by stretching their heads, they hop up for every seed. Insects (ants, termites, flies) are also caught in short spurts of fluttering flight in pursuit of the prey.

## Fear Reactions

You can tell by looking at a Zebra Finch whether it is fearful, agitated, or nervous or whether it is feeling at ease. If a bird is startled by a sound or movement nearby

or if others of the species or predators threaten, the bird immediately makes itself as slim as it can and peers around anxiously. If a Zebra Finch is weaker than an attacker of the same species, it sometimes "surrenders" by assuming the begging posture of fledglings (p. 75). Often the finch does not know in what direction to escape and nervously wags its tail back and forth and twitches its wings. This behavior indicates a desire to fly away, uncertainty, and uneasiness. A contented bird sits on its perch in a comfortable position and occasionally shakes its feathers for relaxation.

## Aggressive Behavior

The charm of Zebra Finches lies in their gregarious ways. But there are fights even in the friendliest society. If a competition arises with a neighbor over food, perches, nesting sites, nesting material, a nest, or the mate, a Zebra Finch responds aggressively to defend its own interests.

The most harmless form this aggression takes—and I have often observed this in my birds—is a craning of the neck forward in such a way that the closed bill and lowered head silently point toward the opponent. If the latter has not strayed near the nest accidentally, a short pecking fight will quickly restore the "rightful" order. If the owner of the nest catches sight of the intruder at a distance, the owner may mount a flying attack and simply push the other bird off the perch. When this happens, a clear cry of anger can be heard.

In a cage that is too small, two Zebra Finches will often fight desperately over the same nesting site even if two nests are hanging there side by side. In this case both birds feel that right is on their side. It can happen that the loser is grabbed by the nape feathers, then drops to the ground as though dead, and is unable to fly up again without fear of renewed attack. In nature and in spacious aviaries such fights are rare.

**Calls and Other Vocalizations**

Zebra Finches can produce quite a range of sounds:

*Contact call:* This short, soft sound is almost constantly audible and forms a background noise familiar to the ears of any owner of Zebra Finches. It helps pairs and groups of birds keep track of each other, but one bird does not answer another.

If this sound is emitted abruptly, more loudly, and more rapidly than usual, it is a warning signal to the other birds that some danger is lurking (p. 47).

*Beckoning call:* This call is drawn out and much louder than the contact call. It serves the same function as the latter when the birds have lost sight of each other. If it is uttered at a higher pitch than usual, it also serves to warn other birds.

*Nest call:* This is a long-drawn-out, soft, whimpering sound that a pair produces when inspecting a nesting site (p. 42).

*Mating cry:* During copulation both partners utter a soft, "quivery" succession of sounds.

*Cry of anger:* Zebra Finches utter a cry of varying loudness before they attack. If you have several pairs of birds and hear that cry often, this is a clear sign that the aviary is too small for its population.

*Cry of fear:* This is a loud, shrill cry that

Male Zebra Finches sing their courtship display songs all year round, even when no females are there to hear them.

I have heard only rarely and only from young birds that were being caught by hand or grabbed by the neck by older Zebra Finches (see "Aggressive Behavior," p. 70).

*Song of the male:* This song is made up of two parts: a series of short, rapid cackling sounds and a loud trill. As part of the courtship display it serves to induce the female to mate, but it is never used in claiming territory (see "Pairing and Courtship," p. 72). At the height of sexual excitement, the male punctuates his song with loud beckoning calls. The songs of the courtship display are sung at all times of year (even if the cock has no mate), a sign that this species of bird is perpetually prepared to breed.

**How Zebra Finches Recognize Each Other**

In order to survive and reproduce, animals have to be able to recognize others of their species and potential sexual partners. Zebra

# Understanding Zebra Finches

Finches do this primarily by sight. They recognize each other instantly by the red color of the bill and the typical black and white pattern of the face. The markings on the head are particularly striking and enable the birds to recognize each other even in the semidark of the nest hollow.

The White Zebra Finches bred in captivity have lost these facial markings and therefore pass over normally colored members of their own kind to favor artificially bred white birds of other *Estrildidae*-species. Initially the only sign by which these White Zebra Finches recognize a partner is the red color of the bill, which is lighter in the female than the male. Later on they can also tell by the voice.

Among wild Zebra Finches the birds recognize each other's sex by the presence or absence of the male's brighter plumage. The hen reacts most directly to the orange cheek spot of the male; this prominent sign is considerably more effective than the markings on the throat and sides, although even these by themselves could trigger mating behavior in the female. The effect of the brown color of the sides is enhanced, by the way, by the white dots. But the colorful plumage of the male serves primarily as a signal to other males. That is why normally colored males always keep at a safe distance from each other, whereas White Zebra Finch cocks do not.

Young Zebra Finches are immediately recognized as members of the species by the tear line running down from the eye. The black beak identifies them as juveniles and thus protects them against the aggressive and sexual urges of the adult birds. White Zebra Finch fledglings again differ from this norm: Their bills turn pink soon after they leave the nest.

Zebra Finches recognize their own mates and offspring by the voice. Pairs that have in the past raised young together immediately recognize each other again even after having been separated for several months, and they will give up bonds formed in the interim. Zebra Finches thus bond permanently.

## Pairing and Courtship

Young, sexually mature Zebra Finches find their mates in the flocks we have already discussed. Usually it is the male who initiates the relationship by singing to a hen and hopping and flying around her. If she finds him compatible, she responds with the same display gestures. But the display ritual proper does not take place until later; the two have to get used to each other first (p. 40).

A complete mating display ritual consists of a five-step sequence. The male starts by flying around the hen and singing to her while showing off the colorful parts of his plumage and turning his tail feathers toward her. The hen responds with lively greetings, involving bowing and pointing her tail feathers in his direction. This in turn causes him to do his courtship dance. He now hops closer, turning 180° at each hop until he arrives, singing, next to her. The hen now hunches down and signals, by vibrating her tail up and down, that she is ready to be mounted. After the mating has taken place, the cock sometimes quivers his tail, too.

# Understanding Zebra Finches

If this sequence is not followed rigidly, no successful mating takes place. Young cocks therefore need time to learn how to proceed.

According to Dr. Matthew M. Vriends, a noted ornithologist, the mating dance in captivity is practically identical: "The dance and the mating can be repeated several times. After mating, the male puts himself into an erect, horizontal position and quivers up and down with his tail—paralleling the behavior of the female. That's why Dr. Morris calls this 'pseudo-female behavior.'

The hen invites the cock to mount her by vibrating her tail up and down.

"Usually the mating dance takes place in dead trees or bushes, because the leaves of living vegetation seem to limit the movements of the birds. Not infrequently, mating even takes place on the ground or on rocks.

"I believe that, in the wild, Zebra Finches mate for life. In captivity, however, the birds don't stay a couple nearly as much. In the wild, the couple stays together the entire year, even if they join a large flock. They live together in a comfortable sleeping nest to which they retire at sunset. At times, they also go into their nest during the day to protect themselves from the intense rays of the Australian sun."

Compared to the normal mating ritual, the courtship behavior of White Zebra Finches exhibits some serious disturbances. A normally colored cock suppresses the flight instinct of the hen by flashing his bright colors at her. But in the case of White Zebra Finches the female immediately flees from the courting male, thus stimulating his aggressive drive so that he either chases her away or rapes her.

The immediate cause of this atypical behavior is not the lack of colorful plumage but rather the early imprinting (p. 48) caused by the presence of both white parents and white siblings. Thus, white females raised by white parents do not even recognize colored cocks as members of the species and consequently flee from them, whereas they do ultimately get personally acquainted with white cocks and learn to appreciate them. White cocks court white hens but will simultaneously chase away or even attack potential mates that are gray, something a gray imprinted male would never do. Gray imprinted cocks sometimes court white cocks mistaking them for hens.

## Brooding and Rearing

Zebra Finches usually nest in low thorny bushes or small trees. Sometims, however, they nest on the ground, in grass clumps, hollow trees, rabbit burrows, and the like. At times they try unusual sites, such as termite hills, the substructures of nests of predatory birds, nests of other grass finches (which are taken over without alterations), and swallow nests. Nests are also found under roofs, in gutters, and in holes in fence posts.

The nest is built from rough grass and is furnished on the inside with soft grass and fluff from fruits. The brooding chamber is lined with feathers, rabbit hair, sheep wool, and fluff. In areas without grass, the birds use thin twigs and roots for the external structure. Nests in bushes and such have been described as "bottle shaped," with the entrance on the side. If Zebra Finches build nests in a hollow, they sometimes don't make a separate roof. Outside the breeding season, Zebra Finches often build a play or sleep nest. It differs from the brooding nest in that it usually doesn't have the "bottle neck," the little entrance tunnel. Yet at times the birds will use old brooding nests for sleeping, according to Dr. Vriends.

Brooding nests are constructed by both partners. Generally the male concentrates on fetching building material, which is used by the female. However, that is not always the case. Dr. Vriends has noticed both sexes in Central Australia, Southwest Australia, and Queensland carrying building materials. He thinks that in those areas both birds work together to finish the nest quickly to take advantage of the rainy season. Normally, when the birds do not rush, completing a nest may take almost two weeks. In Central Australia, Zebra Finches start nest building immediately when the first rains come, irrespective of the season. The reason is that when it rains, vegetation develops, a source of feed for the birds.

The rainy season can be quite short, so that the birds start building nests quickly to be able to raise at least one family before the dry season. In regions with more rain, like Northern Australia, Zebra Finches breed from October to April.

A good clutch consists of three to eight eggs (the normal is four to six). The egg color is light blue to white and the size varies. Dr. Vriends has recorded eggs with these dimensions: $9.83 \times 13.84$ millimeters and $11.7 \times 16.2$ millimeters, which corresponds to an average of $10.7 \times 14.95$ millimeters.

Brooding begins after the fourth or fifth egg is laid, and is done by both sexes. Male and female relieve each other in a way that avoids attracting potential enemies. It is worth noting that the male frequently carries a blade of grass, some fluff, or a feather in his beak, most likely, to incorporate it into the nest edge— perhaps a form of relaxation. The female never does this, as far as Dr. Vriends can determine. At dusk, both partners go into the nest, and by the first morning light, the male leaves.

In the wild, the eggs start hatching after 12½ to 16 days, depending on the weather, and within 36 hours all the nestlings are hatched. At first they are flesh colored with a few white down feathers and a yellowish bill. In the course of the next few days the bill and the body turn black. On the seventh day the primaries erupt, on the tenth day the tail feathers, and one or two days after that the smaller contour feathers. On the twelfth day the vanes on the primaries become visible. By the time the fledglings

# Understanding Zebra Finches

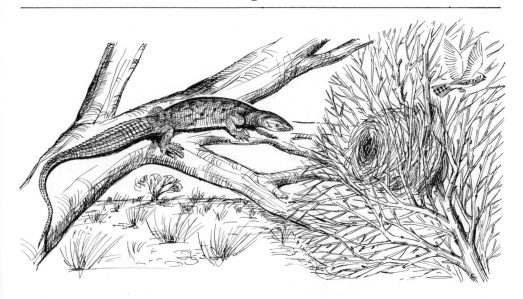

Nest robbers, like this monitor lizard, are the Zebra Finches' most dangerous enemies.

are ready to leave the nest their plumage is complete.

Zebra Finch babies have a specific pattern of dark dots on light on the inside of the bill and on the tongue (a common trait in *Estrildidae*-species) that triggers feeding behavior in the parent birds. At first the fledglings simply raise their heads when they are hungry; later they assume the typical begging posture of twisting the neck, a posture that is also observed outside the nest (p. 44).

Zebra Finches are at least 22 days old when they first try to fly. During the next few days the parents still feed them in the nest, to which they lure the young back.

This behavior is called "nest guiding." This is the time when parents and offspring learn to recognize each other by voice. As soon as the young birds learn to find and hull seeds on their own, they start moving about the entire brood colony. There they meet other groups of young birds with whom they now spend time, because their parents return to the flock for hours at a time. In the evening the juvenile birds return to their brooding nests or to one of the sleeping nests, usually together with their parents. In this regard, Dr. Vriends made the following observation: "The male has a funny way of making sure that his offspring disappear into a (sleeping) nest at night: he often has something enticing in his beak to lure the young ones to bed. More sleeping nests are often constructed, if needed. In Queensland I have observed males in the evening with termites in their beaks, directing the young ones into different nests. As far as I could tell, the fathers were not particularly concerned whether it was just their own brood or some others that they bundled off to sleep. One Zebra Finch, for example, brought 12 young to different nests, although he himself was the father of just four! During beautiful summer weather with hot days, aviary males may direct the little ones not to sleeping nests, but rather to a protected spot or strong branch in the aviary. In the wild, however, sleeping nests are always used. When the male has chosen a suitable spot, you must be very sure no cats or other bird enemies can get near it. For this reason double screening is highly recommended.''

During the sixth week the black bill starts to change color, turning red in about two weeks. The juvenile molt begins at this point and is completed when the birds are about three months old. At the conclusion of this molt the female birds are sexually mature. The males have to wait another two weeks. This staggered timing precludes matings among siblings, because in nature the young, sexually mature females quickly find older mates. The rapid sexual maturing of Zebra Finches is an adaptation to the unpredictable breeding times preceding or following rainy periods. It also helps compensate for population losses due to inclement weather, predator birds, and nest robbers like lizards, snakes, and honeyeaters (a kind of bird).

## Consequences of Domestication

The Zebra Finch has become a popular cage bird in our century. Since these birds reproduce easily in captivity, people stopped importing wild ones from Australia quite early. In addition, Australia passed strict laws in 1960 prohibiting the export of native fauna. During this extended segregation from their wild relatives, domesticated Zebra Finches have developed differences in appearance and behavior. The most striking of these are the many deliberately bred changes in color and the difference in size between wild and domesticated strains. Modifications in behavior, some of which you are already familiar with, are less obvious. They include:

• shorter time for nest building and incubation.

• accelerated development (reaching full color and sexual maturity) of the young.

• quicker succession of broods.

• behavioral disturbances in White Zebra Finches (p. 73).
Further signs of degeneration are:

• exaggerated sexual drive, which, particularly in small cages, goes hand in hand with curtailment of the courtship ritual (p. 49). The birds engage in a great deal of courtship behavior but do not carry it through to completion.

• tendency on the part of some cocks to court males of other *Estrildidae* species.

• exaggerated urge for nest building that

can interfere with the regular brooding process.

• irregular brooding and feeding of the nestlings.

• increased need for contact, which can get in the way of the birds taking turns sitting on the eggs. It can also lead to a diminishing of the distance cocks keep from each other (p. 72).

• inability to distinguish between their own young and those of other species on the basis of the pattern inside the oral cavity. Zebra Finches are therefore often used as foster parents to raise the young of other *Estrildidae*-species, but these young are then generally unusable for further breeding (p. 48).

Such results of long-term domestication occur more frequently in the unusual color strains than in Gray Zebra Finches. The prime cause for these changes lies no doubt in unnatural selection of the breeding stock, that is, selection based on human whim. That is why I plead for preserving the natural appearance and behavior of Zebra Finches.

# Index

# Index

# Index